S0-AEJ-254

The Behavioral Sciences:

Essays in Honor of George A. Lundberg

The Behavioral Sciences: Essays in Honor of GEORGE A. LUNDBERG

edited by

ALFRED DE GRAZIA
ROLLO HANDY
E. C. HARWOOD
PAUL KURTZ

published by

The Behavioral Research Council
Great Barrington, Massachusetts

Preface

This volume of collected essays is dedicated to the memory of George A. Lundberg. It is fitting that this volume is published under the auspices of the Behavioral Research Council. George Lundberg, as its first President, and one of its founding members, was dedicated to the goals of the Behavioral Research Council: namely, the encouragement and development of behavioral science research and its application to the problems of men in society.

He has been a constant inspiration to behavioral research not only in sociology, where he was considered to be a classic figure and a major influence but in the behavioral sciences in general.

Part One of this volume includes papers on George Lundberg and his scientific work, particularly in the field of sociology. Originally read at a special conference of the Pacific Sociological Association (March 30-April 1, 1967), the papers are here published by permission of the Society.

Part Two contains papers not directly on George Lundberg but on themes and topics close to his interest. They are written by members of the Behavioral Research Council.

We hope that this volume is a token, however small, of the profound contribution that George Lundberg has made to the development of the behavioral sciences. We especially wish to thank the contributors of the George A. Lundberg Memorial Fund, particularly those at the University of Washington, who have made this volume possible.

The Editors
Alfred de Grazia
Rollo Handy
E. C. Harwood
Paul Kurtz

Table of Contents

PART I

Lundberg's Encounters with Sociology and Vice Versa

OTTO N. LARSEN
University of Washington

INTRODUCTION

This paper presents some biographical and autobiographical notes on the career of the late George A. Lundberg, notes that tell us something of how this man developed his sociological interests and his professional style.

George Lundberg's encounters with sociology—indeed, his encounters with all of life—were vigorous, searching, sensitive, intelligent, and highly productive of wit and wisdom.

He loved the battlefield of the intellect, but he always respected the skills and the rights of his adversaries. He studied leisure objectively, but not to the exclusion of practicing it with an abundant grace. He frequently cast himself into the role of agitator and polemicist not only to defend sociology against alleged enemies, camp followers, and traducers, but also because, as he once wrote Howard Odum, "polemics and controversial writing require relatively little time and provide some legitimate amusement in an academic career."

Here, then, was a life and a career that brought verve and vitality to the social and to the sociological scene. To have encountered George Lundberg in either place is to grow curious about the forces that nourished and brought forth his brilliant range of qualities.

By 1961, the year of his retirement from teaching, I could contain my curiosities no longer and I undertook a campaign to persuade him to write, in effect, the story of his sociological life. At first, Lundberg was skeptical about the merit of an autobiographical project. In part, I think, this reflected his feeling that a self-conscious recounting for posterity may in itself distort the record. Furthermore, he was uncomfortable about anything that symbolized old age. He preferred anticipations of the future to reminiscences of the past. In his thoughts, actions, and associations he was consistently youth-oriented and youthful in outlook. He also had a desire to allocate the new time he had gained in early retirement from teaching to other projects such as editing the McKay Social Science Series, re-exploring human ecology, and taking his son to baseball games.

Gradually, however, an autobiographical project took shape. He responded favorably to the proposal that he select a number of his published papers, classify them into a limited set of themes—such as the natural science trend in sociology, values, sociometry, surveys and case methods, polemics, etc.—and write introductions to each section telling how his interests in that line of work developed. In one of our many exchanges of notes, he wrote: "Your support, not to say coercion, is impossible to resist. I agree that a study of sociologists at work and a report on obstacles, plans, successes and frustrations can itself be a contribution to the science we are seeking to develop. I take it that the task is to specify something about why and how my career developed as it did. I'll want to think carefully about the state and development of sociology during the period 1920-1960. It was high drama with many actors. I was lucky to have a small part in the play and to sense a little sooner than some what the probable outcome had to be. The notes and anecdotes on events and episodes will be easy to collect, but hard to select. Actually I was involved in some pretty good scraps, but some great cooperative efforts too. After I get these fragments together we'll try to fit them into a pattern to illuminate larger intellectual and organizational issues. I might enjoy this after all."

Lundberg then began the task, one that failing health impeded but one that he talked about and worked on to the very closing hours of his life. Unfortunately he did not complete the work, leaving untouched major sections such as his encounter with the issue of values in science about which he was puzzled as to how his position could be so misunderstood. What he left behind were notes and fragments on personal experiences that were later to be fitted into an interpretive commentary. From these, I want to bring you some of the reflections of a man whose encounters with sociology left their mark on the field. What follows are his thoughts edited from his last papers.

INTO SOCIOLOGY THROUGH EDUCATION

Most of my life has been spent in education—as student, teacher, high school principal, school superintendent, and college professor. As I look back to the beginning I find this somewhat remarkable since, by today's standards, my academic career was not launched in a manner particularly promising of survival let alone any measure of success. My earliest years, about the turn of the century, were typical of the children of "covered wagon" parents, and, in view of the excellent stories that have been published portraying life on the evolving prairie country, it would be superfluous to repeat another account here.[1] Suffice it to say there was usually lots of hard labor, plenty to eat, but a dearth of reading matter. In the latter connection, I know I speak for thousands of my generation when I acknowledge with deep gratitude the stimulating influence of the periodic catalogs of *Sears Roebuck* and *Montgomery Ward.* I still regard them as valuable reference books for students of social and technological change.

My formal training began with eight years in a one-room schoolhouse. My route to higher academic training was somewhat irregular. I did not attend high school. There were no high schools

[1] I especially recommend as relevant in my case, O. E. Rolvaag, *Giants in the Earth,* and Sophus K. Winther, *Take All to Nebraska.*

within convenient traveling distance of our farm home in North Dakota. Furthermore, farm boys were in urgent demand as participants in the pre-mechanical farm economy, and that economy provided little money for higher educational purposes, especially in a large family. Actually, these handicaps were blessings in disguise. They compelled me to take a College Preparatory Course from a Chicago correspondence school, which, I found out later, was so superior to what was offered by the regular high schools of the time and place as to make my subsequent college career a very easy matter.

By teaching country school for a livelihood and devoting spare time to the corespondence course, I was able, after a couple of years to enter the state university. Administrators in that admirable but over-conscientious institution caused me much more trouble on account of the "unconventional" character of my preparatory work than did the content of the various courses. However, after innumerable special examinations and other maneuvers, I was finally allowed to enter and to graduate in the School of Education.

This took place after a fifteen-months' interruption for service in the First World War. The trip to France was not particularly notable, but the extended demobilization period in England afforded a number of unique opportunities. In fact, my connection with World War I was to me personally an adventure excellently timed and adapted to both World Wars. I escaped most of the irritations, indignities, and absurdities of the military routine and felt more than adequately repaid for the inconvenience by a three-month's period of study at the London School of Economics. This was an arrangement by which the more literate American soldiers were invited to spend part of their time while waiting for transportation back to the U.S.A. The sojourn in London with practically no obligations at all was an unqualified pleasure. The opera and the theater were going full blast, and I took full advantage of them. At the University, Hobhouse lectured on moral philosophy and Westermarck on The Family. I also took advantage of other offerings in economics, history, and politics.

Upon returning home from Europe, I continued in Education as a career. This was in part a hedge against unemployment, but I was also to enjoy two years of high school teaching and small-town school administration. My career at this level of education ended abruptly with the following incident:

In 1920 I was notified by telephone of my appointment as Superintendent of schools of Hope, North Dakota. In the interval between this telephone conversation and the arrival of the confirming letter, the attention of the Board of Education had been called to my alleged sympathies for the Non-Partisan League. Thereupon, the Board withdrew from their contract forthwith. I demanded a hearing, which was granted.

There were no facts in dispute, or at least both sides disdained to resort to them. All felt that High Principle was really the issue. The Board made no allegations regarding my membership or activity on my part on behalf of the League, and I offered no apologies for my political and economic views. Neither party appealed to any laws, regulations, or rules governing the dismissal of teachers in North Dakota at this time. The whole proceeding was carried on in an air of moral grandeur that was awe-inspiring.

The meeting was opened by the president of the Board of Education, whom I shall call Mr. Blank from here on. Mr. Blank was also president of the First National Bank in the parlor of which we met. I shall give only the verdict and its justification. In his role of judge, prosecutor, and Pontifex Maximus, Mr. Blank intoned as follows: "I don't think it would be proper" he said, "for this Board to ask whether you are a Methodist or a Presbyterian; but we do think that we have a right to ask, 'Are you a Christian?' In the same way, it would never occur to this Board to ask whether you are a Republican or a Democrat. But we do think we have a right to ask you, 'Are you a Socialist?' "

Curiously, I have no vivid recollection of subsequent discussion. Perhaps Mr. Blank's logic was so overwhelming as to paralyze further talk.

A job for the ensuing year became my major concern. It was late in the season. At the last moment a call came that was to take me from the public schools *forever* and lodge me in college and university life for just as long. With one appointment I became professor of psychology and education as well as sociology at a small church college in Nebraska. The record shows that I was also Director of the Teacher Training Department at this earnest little institution.

INTO SOCIOLOGY THROUGH REFORM

My early interest in sociology may be attributed in part to a very strong "action" and reform drive derived from living in an immigrant community. This community consisted almost 100 percent of the "refugees" (Scandinavian, Russian, German) from the petty tyrannies of the "upper" classes in Europe, from religious persecution, from military service, and from economic destitution. This situation was heavily reinforced by endless stories and songs of the "class struggle" in the homelands of the emigrants and a fierce delight in their relative liberation, even though their economic hardships continued to oppress them. Accordingly, these were the first objectives of reform. The story of the Non-Partisan League, a farmer's political reform organization, is the best illustration of the beginning of "political consciousness" in this era.

As far as I personally was concerned, I was very much a part of this picture. Among the dramatic personal incidents which influenced me should be mentioned that at some point when I was about ten or twelve years of age I acquired, somehow, a copy of Victor Hugo's *Les Miserables*. I cannot remember how I got the notion I wanted it or how I got my hands on it, though the answer to the second question is almost certainly, Sears Roebuck. Suffice it to say that nothing before or since so ignited my reform pressures as did Victor Hugo's masterpiece. I still read its first part with deep emotion.

The additional influence of Professor J. M. Gillette was conclusive. To save the contemporary Valjeans became my life's Number One Project. I signed all petition for release of all political prisoners defended by the *Nation* and *The New Republic*. Gillette doubtless counseled me that, given my objective, sociology, and more particularly criminology, was the clear indication. I now had a cause, a challenge, a purpose, and even a considerable reputation as a radical. In short, I felt fine.

I signed up for an M.A. *in absentia* (residence for three summers) at Wisconsin where Professors Ross, Gillin, *et al.* were in great and deserved demand. They taught a highly moralistic brand of sociology which was quite congenial to me at the time, but they paid more than usual attention to facts. The teaching was good and the required reading was excellent. Veblen's *Theory of the Leisure Class* was a delight—I had not encountered this kind of objectivity before. I had great admiration for McDougall's *Social Psychology,* but I also enjoyed its complete demolition a year later at the hands of L. L. Bernard. *Justice and the Poor* was another title, and it appeared for a time that I might have to become a lawyer—the poor in Boston and elsewhere were in desperate need of Justice as well as of material things. Cooley's *Human Nature and the Social Order* was just the right capstone for this reading. It remains incomparable.

Following the M.A. at Wisconsin, I then secured a teaching fellowship at the University of Minnesota and decided to pursue the Ph.D., although that was regarded both by myself and my home community as "a lot of nerve" for a person with my background.

SEEING SOCIOLOGY AS A SCIENCE

Apart from my inability to avoid the temptation to indulge in sideswipes at current topics, perhaps the general theme most prominently associated with my work is that of the natural science trend in sociology. An account of how my interests emerged in this area can best begin by briefly recalling the relevant intellectual tides of the 1920's. I believe it is fair to say that at the time under consideration (ca. 1920-1925), sociology was still, on its theoretical side, a philosophical subject stressing ethics and a moral appraisal of contemporary events. On the applied side, sociology was confused with social work, "surveys," and reform. This was also a time when a dozen or more states enacted, or considered, laws forbidding the teaching of the doctrine of *evolution* even in the universities, as well as in the secondary and lower schools. Add to these cross-winds the emerging revolution of *relativity* in the natural sciences, and we find an intellectual era that was trying to pull itself together after two of the most important intellectual upheavals in history, namely, Darwinism and relativity, neither of which has, as yet, spent its full sociological force.

The decline of the "instinct" approach and the popularity of behaviorism further cleared the deck for later departures.[2] Under the circumstances, it was perhaps more or less inevitable that in casting about for a satisfactory orientation, the natural science approach would find increasing appeal among the younger social scientists. The result was a pronounced swing toward empiricism, of all degrees of "rawness."

The transition to more rigorous methods and objective standards was not without resistance in many quarters. When I began my graduate work at the University of Wisconsin, John R. Commons was chairman of the combined Departments of Economics and Sociology. One of the requirements for the Master's degree in both fields was a course in elementary statistics. I remember having quite an argument with Professor Commons regarding this requirement, because, I argued, statistics had no relevance to sociology, and therefore should not be required of sociology students. Commons would not even argue the point. He merely said, "No." The result was that I struggled through W. I. King's *Elements of Statistics,* plus a laboratory period and lectures. After prodigious labors I finally managed to pass the course with a "C" and with a solemn vow to have nothing further to do with this truly dismal science.

This episode may be of some interest to those who have wondered how I became so rabid a disciple of a doctrine and a method in which I myself had so ignominious a background. The principal influences which I recall vividly are Karl Pearson's *Grammar of Science,* and the combined influence of F. Stuart Chapin, L. L. Bernard, and M. C. Elmer. Their work left little doubt in my

[2] Part of the story I have reviewed in "Quantitative Methods in Sociology: 1920-1960," *Social Forces,* October, 1960, pp. 19-24.

mind as to the scientific future of sociology. After ruefully reconsidering the whole matter, I reluctantly undertook a statistical seminar project, under Bernard, which developed into my first full-length paper for the *American Journal of Sociology*.[3] I soon found statistical methods a fascinating as well as an indispensable subject. My first book (*Social Research,* 1929) bears witness to the thoroughness of my conversion.

In the meantime I became a sort of John the Baptist crying in the wilderness regarding greater men than I coming soon to demonstrate the wonders of the doctrine itself. In addition, I did, however, spend a post-doctoral summer at Columbia in a desperate attempt to remedy the worst of my shortcomings in this field, until such time as I could turn over the subject to subordinates more competent than myself. In the meantime I continued to preach the basic gospel, and to experiment with some new indexes and coefficients in sociometric work.

SURVEYS AND POLLING

During the 1920's and 30's it was discovered by sociologists, psychologists, and other social scientists that "interesting" articles could be written reporting upon the attitudes of students and the general public on all manners of questions, but usually including some inquiry regarding sex, crime, the family, God, and other assorted subjects. This was the golden "research" era before reliable interviewing, sampling, probability theory and Chi-squares were used. These preliminary descriptive studies were well worth their cost as part of the improvement in the technique of scale and questionnaire construction to follow later in the important work of men like Stouffer, Lazarsfeld, and Guttman. Indeed, one of the most significant developments during the thirties was the advancement in techniques for measuring public opinion. But in the meantime the questionnaire flourished in many

[3] "The Demographic and Economic Basis of Political Radicalism and Conservatism," *American Journal of Sociology,* March, 1927, pp. 719-732. This paper was motivated by my interest in the Farmer's Non-Partisan League, which has flourished in the Middle West for several decades, and is still a political force of some proportion.

primitive forms. On completing my graduate work I hastened to seize upon the large "captive" sections of "Soc. One" to exploit them for their views on "social issues." The results were tabulated to compare males with females, and the percentage answering yes or no to each question. The report on the study was promptly accepted for publication in an educational journal, my first article in print.[4] The students, of course, were eager to know the extent of their ideological deviation from the norms.[5]

An incident connected with this study should be mentioned in passing. Two of the questions in our schedule were these:

"Is it right to kiss a man or woman you do not expect to marry?"	Yes———	No———
"Was the Bible verbally inspired by God?"	Yes———	No———

The secretary of the university president sent me some clippings from a remote Canadian town with a note reading as follows: "Here is the type of (unfavorable) publicity we are getting from your questionnaire study."

With the indignation of a new Asssistant Professor, I replied that the study had been undertaken on the initiative and full consent of the Dean of Men and was not regarded as unpermissible even by his office. It looked for a while like a small case of "academic freedom," and I wondered if I was about to become a hero. But the President (Suzzalo) threw cold water on the whole episode in a handwritten note as follows: "Go ahead with your study—don't worry too much about the publicity."

This sort of thing became quite common during the 30's and caused some wrangling about academic freedom. The question was whether a professor in the name of research could circulate questionnaires on any subject no matter how it might embarrass the university's public relations. In the meantime, the public attitude toward such questions seemed to undergo a change in the

[4] "Sex Differences on Social Questions," *School and Society,* May 8, 1926, pp. 595-600.

[5] My colleague, Read Bain, collaborated in this empirical study and made a separate analysis, published elsewhere, of that part of the questionnaire dealing with religion.

direction of reduced sensitivity. Improved understanding and experience with questionnaire studies, e.g., in the army, the Kinsey Report, and others may have helped. At any rate, I experienced no further difficulties of this type.

I first encountered and participated in field studies and survey research at the University of Minnesota where M. C. Elmer was teaching courses and writing texts on the subject and F. Stuart Chapin's 1920 book on *Field Work and Social Research* represented an attempt to raise the scientific standards of this type of empirical inquiry. (See also my *Social Research,* 2nd edition, 1942, Ch. XI).

My first teaching assignment (at the University of Washington) was a sequence of three quarter-courses, listed respectively as Social Surveys, Social Statistics, and Social Exhibits. The logic of the sequence was to follow the natural order of inquiry; namely, (1) to make relevant observations, (2) to analyze them statistically and systematically, and (3) to exhibit the results. I was more or less familiar with the first two topics but found the third field somewhat undeveloped, to say the least. So I taught some more statistics and statistical graphics. In connection with the latter, I was fortunate in having as a student Calvin F. Schmid who was subsequently to become a leading authority on this and other related subjects. I undertook also during the summer of 1925 a survey of certain aspects of child life in Tacoma, a one-man project of which part was published in booklet form by the Rotary Club of Tacoma in 1926 under the title *Child Life in Tacoma.* It was important chiefly as a further installment on my education. I discovered that for the health aspects of the survey the American Public Health Association had already developed an objective rating scale for city health work. The idea that such standards might also be established for other aspects of urban and rural life was quite exciting and engaged a good deal of my attention for about ten years (1930-1940). At the end of that period I had published two papers on the measurement of socio-economic status.

The depression of the 1930's, and the later war years, greatly stimulated further "social surveys" and other short-term research for federal agencies like the Federal Emergency Relief Administration (FERA). Adequately trained personnel was the great need. Many a recent assistant professor found himself over night a "director" or "supervisor" of field projects and other large-scale research beyond his training and experience. However, what the work frequently lacked in scientific sophistication was made up in enthusiasm for the task. Thousands of individuals poured into Washington on short notice to work under most difficult conditions for almost entirely patriotic reasons. I shall confine myself to a simple illustration which was reported to me by the "case" himself. A well-known professor happened to be downtown one afternoon when the newspapers ran headlines reporting a new study and the usual shortage in trained personnel. Without further preparation, my "case," in his shirt sleeves and without luggage of any kind, dashed to the nearest railroad station (no air space available) and in fifteen minutes was on his way to Washington.

Comparison and jokes about experiences of this kind became common cocktail conversation, as also did anecdotes regarding scientific and statistical short-cuts that someone had allegedly practiced, or reported that a rival or hostile agency had practiced. Among such reports was a rumor that a new method of sampling was in use, to wit: See that every congressional district is represented by at least one person. Sociologists had to learn to recognize *politically* as well as mathematically "valid" sampling.

In 1934 I became supervisor of one of those studies, although I already had one job at Columbia (an evening lecture course and a recreation survey of Westchester County) and another at Bennington, Vermont. By the way, this form of moonlighting was very common during the depression and later during the War.

It seems that practically anyone within train or air commuting distance was eligible for a job in Washington. In typical emergency fashion, I was summoned by telephone in the late afternoon, at Bennington, by a person in Washington, D.C., whom I had never heard of before. He outlined by telephone somewhat vaguely in barest outline what the whole project was about—a nationwide survey of the Occupational Characteristics of the Urban Unemployed, data to be gathered and analyzed by a stipulated date (a matter of weeks) for the information of a Congressional committee —and could I come to Washington on a night train to take charge of this small chore?

Well, I could, and did. After all, these were exciting times. I was much interested in my leisure study in Westchester County but—it was *not* part of a national emergency and this was a matter of some importance at the time. Anyway, I went to Washington on a part-time basis, all details to be arranged.

After about five days, I still had not seen the people in charge in Washington. (I am speaking now of the depression rather than of the War, although the social psychology of the era was much the same.) Now, however, an executive called on me and we left the office together. He explained we would go for an automobile ride in Virginia because it had been found impossible to have a talk any other way. I pumped him as intensively as I dared (he was under great nervous strain from overwork and lack of sleep). There remained what almost wrecked the plans for the survey, namely, some person in authority to specify *what were the purposes, the aims, the objectives of it all?* Harry Hopkins was in charge of FERA at the time and it would normally be his function to specify the general purposes of the study. The higher directors, however, seemed to have the idea that since I had been brought in to have charge of the study, I should also tell them what the study ought to tell the executives as to what they *ought to want.* Finally, it seems that someone cornered Hopkins in the elevator of the Walker-Johnson Building and insisted that he specify in writing the questions for which they wanted answers. This Hopkins finally did on the back of an old envelope. We immediately went to work on a night-and-day schedule for information to be gathered. Not a bad study altogether as I recall it.

SOCIOMETRY

About the same time that opinion-polling techniques began to be structured in a serious scientific way, some allied techniques for objectifying the observation of other highly relevant social phenomena came onto the scene, sparked by the lively genius of J. L. Moreno. From the point of empiricism, the introduction of *sociometry* during the 1930's was very important because it boldly invaded the happy hunting grounds of traditional sociology, namely, inter-personal relationships *per se*.

Throughout its early history, the "inner essence" of sociology was emphasized as was the alleged inaccessibility of this "inner" realm to the ordinary method of science. Sociometry, through the medium of language and what came to be called sociometric testing (analysis of verbal reactions to simple question of likes and dislikes) helped open up and objectify a large area of important phenomena which had hitherto largely been subject only to imaginative and subjective approaches. From the start, much of the appeal of sociometry could also be traced to the fact that many found in its techniques useful applications to various practical problems. Consider the following quotation from J. L. Moreno:

> Dr. Frank Wilson, Minister of the Episcopal Church of Hyde Park, a regular visitor at the New York State Training School for Girls at Hudson, after reading *Who Shall Survive?* decided to make sociometry the theme of a Sunday sermon. President Roosevelt, who was in the church that morning, became interested. Dr. Wilson invited me to meet the President next Sunday in his church. The President sat in the first row of pews, I sat in the last and when the religious ceremony was over Mr. Roosevelt had to pass my seat. Suddenly he stopped and said: "Hello, Dr. Moreno," as if he would know me. He invited me into his car; on his lap he had a copy of *Who Shall Survive?* He opened it and pointed at one of the sociograms. "This looks like progressive sociology," he said, and added pensively, "if I would not have taken my present course, this is the kind of thing I would have liked to do." He further stated, "When I am back in Washington I will see where your ideas can be put to use." As a matter of fact, sociological leaders like Dr. Charles P. Loomis and Carl C. Taylor, connected with the Department of Agriculture, had already begun to apply these ideas to subsistence homestead projects. I thought that President Roosevelt might forget our meeting

but his interest created a new enthusiasm in Washington which culminated in a large number of sociometric community studies.[6]

The above episode is of interest from several points of view. In the first place, it reflects a laudable openmindedness and hospitality to new ideas on the part of the President who incurred the criticism that it involved an unwarranted waste of time to give audience to all sorts of persons who were eager to present their schemes (usually short-cuts and quick solutions). In fact, Roosevelt once stated that he looked forward to the daily mail with the feeling that perhaps today was the *big* day on which a simple and satisfactory solution was discovered. In short, innovators and cultists "never had it so good" as during the early years of the New Deal. The incident also illustrates the fact that when scientific guidelines are not available, even the conscientious statesman or leader grasps at straws in the hope that some kind of solution will "turn up." The resulting confusion is what is frequently called "muddling thru." Even "muddling thru" is justification when nothing else is available. But trial-and-error is still the most inefficient and costly method.

Sociometry represented an improvement over crude trial-and-error techniques, and owes much of its prowess to a recognition that here was a promising technique for objectifying large areas hitherto regarded as "too subjective" for scientific handling.

I, like Roosevelt, was also impressed with Moreno's ideas, but for additional reasons, reasons that I spelled out in an editorial printed in the February, 1941, edition of *Sociometry*. My attraction to sociometric thinking was evident fairly early. I think my unsolicited review of Moreno's *Who Shall Survive?* in the *A.S.R.* was one of the first to call the attention of the sociological fraternity to his work. My paper on "Social Attraction Patterns in a Village," a project I worked on for three years, and, incidentally, my most cited and reprinted paper, appeared in the first volume of *Sociometry,* then under the editorship of Gardner Murphy. I succeeded

[6] The paragraph here quoted is taken from J. L. Moreno, *Who Shall Survive?* p. lxvi.

Murphy as editor of the journal and served in that capacity for six years. My editorial contacts with Moreno, Murphy, Jennings, Stouffer, Lazarsfeld, Cottrell, Burgess, Loomis, Murdock, Chapin, Zeleny, Dodd, Zipf, Stewart, Sewell, Criswell and others engaged in sociometric inquiry more than compensated for the onerous editorial chore. I confess a special delight in having a hand in opening a column for Read Bain. Starting with the November, 1942, issue of *Sociometry,* and for a number of issues thereafter, Bain ran a remarkable series of columns under the title, "Man is the Measure. . . ." As editor, I prepared, but never published, the following note to warn the brethren of the impending delights about to descend on us all:

> During the past five years the readers of the *American Sociological Review* have been considerably regaled and relieved from the stern tone of the scholarly journals by the editorial comments on men and affairs by Read Bain. On his retirement from the editorship of the *Review,* we suggested to him that he should continue his columnist activities in *Sociometry*. This he has consented to do. Accordingly, we announce herewith a new feature, the nature of which is set forth by the contributor himself. From his opening remarks I conclude that Professor Bain intends to consider himself a *calumnist* rather than a *columnist,* but in any case we welcome his contribution and assure him of freedom from editorial restraint. Barring libel, blasphemy, profanity and sedition, we invite his sage observations on the scientific scene and on the cosmic joke in general. Our columnist has stated so well the reasons for this departure in scholarly journalism that further editorial introduction is unnecessary. Common probity, based on long familiarity with the new columnist's verbal antics and mordent wit, however, dictates that the editors disclaim any responsibility for the views expressed in this column. Also, we specifically reserve the right not to take notice of such of its remarks as are directed at us, without the implication that silence gives approval or admission that we are in any degree at a loss for adequate answer. With this understanding we welcome the premiere columns of scientific journalism.

The tone of this statement perhaps suggests something of the special flavor of the long-standing Lundberg-Bain relationship, a story too rich in detail to detain us here. More important, I use the statement to indicate my conscious hospitality of polemics from any quarters, including, of course, my own—a subject to which I now turn.

A POLEMIC ON POLEMICS

A glance at my General Bibliography will indicate that not all of the items listed are scientific monographs nor even on scientific subjects, although a considerable number falls in the closely related fields of history and philosophy of science. Perhaps a dozen of the nonscientific papers are best classified, in whole or in part, as polemics. They are controversial and disputatious essays on contemporary foreign policy, peace, war, the national interest, semantics, minorities, values, ethics, and even architecture.

Some of my colleagues profess to find this kind of writing, especially for me, a considerable incongruity. Why, it is asked, don't I follow my own advice and maintain a rigorously scientific and detached attitude on *all* things at *all* times? The best answer I can give is to quote some personal correspondence on the subject with the late professor William F. Ogburn, whose urbanity as a scholar and a gentleman was such that, from him, even a rebuke was an honor. I had apparently sent him some minor papers on the polemic variety (perhaps book reviews) which he acknowledged as follows:

July 29, 1948

Dear George:

I appreciate the book and articles on Beard, Morgenstern, and the general subject of our entrance into the war. I find myself in agreement with much that you say and it is a pleasure to find somebody who can see the other side.

However, may I make the following comments:

1. It seems to me that in the material you sent me you deal only with a limited aspect of the subject.
2. That you write as an intellectual rather than a scientist.

You have had, I think much experience in polemics, but to me these articles would have been more effective if your language had been a little less extreme.

Thanks for sending them.

Cordially yours,
Will Ogburn

To which I replied:

August 3, 1948

Dear Will Ogburn:

I think you characterized the material which I sent you somewhat more highly than I do myself when you say that I write as an intellectual rather than as a scientist. I consider this type of writing simply as journalism which in turn is a form of art, which for me again is a kind of recreation. As you know, I feel that the intellectual activities of man can be most satisfactorily classified as science or art, although I may mean by that pretty much what you mean by your distinction between the intellectual and the scientist. In any event, I remember very well the paper in which you first expounded that idea, or at least it was the first time I heard you do it.

The above view also takes care of your first objection, namely, that I deal only with a limited aspect of the subject. This, again, I find to be one of the privileges of journalism and other art and is perhaps what makes it so recreational. I have often said to my classes that I am scientific only about one-hundredth part of my time (incidentally, I think I stole that idea from you) and then chiefly when I am paid for it. The rest of the time I indulge in the luxury of exploiting my likes and dislikes and prejudices regarding things pretty much like ordinary men everywhere do. The rigors of the scientific quest are as yet for the most part, I think, uncongenial to man, being very recent development in his evolution. Nonscientific writing is relatively irresponsible and therefore congenial. This idea does not communicate very easily, however, and a great many of my colleagues as a result are constantly belaboring me because since I have written a good deal about the need for rigorousness and impartiality in scientific method, it seems to be assumed that I must also practice the advice when I am off duty as well as on. I reject the requirement and insist on my right to indulge in harmless recreations like writing for the popular journals, and airing my prejudices as is the privilege of other men.

Incidentally, it (i.e., journalism) is a very easy type of writing and takes almost no time as compared with scientific writing.* I have been working for years on a certain index problem which is only now beginning to clear up. The results will appear only in a doctor's thesis and two or three scholarly papers in obscure journals. Polemic writings may be tossed off at odd intervals by dictation on a machine with perhaps one subsequent correction and retyping. The latter are likely to be read by a much wider audience and the impression results that nearly all of one's production and all of one's time is spent on matters of this kind. I suppose not more than one-half or one-third of the titles in my bibliography consist of what I would regard as empirical and responsible scientific writing. Yet these titles have taken perhaps 98 per cent of the time. And so it goes.

I agree with you also, that my polemics would frequently be more effective if my language were less extreme. But it wouldn't be as much fun to write that way. It's like playing handball more violently than is required to win. It just feels good.

Cordially yours,
George A. Lundberg

* P.S. This is not to imply that great works of art (including journalism) may not be as time consuming and recreational as scientific work of corresponding quality.

His reply contained just three sentences:

August 25, 1948

Dear George:

Your letter on scientific writing was quite engaging. I agree with you 100%.

My latest stunt is writing under an assumed name when I want to have fun.

With all good wishes,
Will Ogburn

In general, my position regarding scientists writing on non-scientific subjects was contained in another letter written about the same time to Professor Howard Odum, who was writing his *American Sociologists* at the time. He had circulated a fairly comprehensive questionnaire to ex-presidents of the American Sociological Association, asking their views on many subjects including the one here under discussion. My reply (in part) was as follows:

> The situation in sociology when I came on the scene was such that the normal course of events frequently projected me into the role of crusader, agitator, and a leader of a faction. Consider the rapid development of quantitative methods, "case studies," social science and values, etc. To undertake scientific work in a jungle, it may be necessary first to hack out, through other than scientific work, a clearing for a cabin in which scientists can work. It may be necessary occasionally to widen that clearing, and finally take an occasional potshot against the former inhabitants of the area who hang around the periphery disturbing or interfering with one's scientific work. I conceive of my polemic writing as of this nature. Similar forays are occasionally necessary against those who try to make social science a tail to some particular political, economic, or sectarian kite. Someone has to do this dirty work in order that scientists, and especially students, may have the opportunity to work unhampered by such distractions. I shall continue to make such discursions when I think it desirable, whether they are considered polemics or not.

The above remarks should not be taken to mean that fun is the only motive for polemic writing. Protracted and illuminating dispute *about* science has been common in the history of science. To take only a single example, Huxley's polemics in support of Darwin and the theory of evolution were as earnestly and soberly motivated as any of the scientists' reports of the development of the theory down to the present time. Indeed, the distinction between polemics and other writing is probably largely a matter of literary style more than anything else. Also, the two categories are not so sharply defined as they are assumed to be. In popular current usage a paper or a speech is categorized as "a polemic" if it is disputatious and argumentative (and advanced by an opponent whom we don't like), as contrasted with the ideal impartial style of a scientific report, in its formulation of hypotheses, selection of valid and representative data, and its avoidance of unwarranted conclusions. Each style of writing has its own purposes, characteristics and value. Perhaps that is all that needs to be said on the subject. Different authors have designated each type by different words. Thus Professor Ogburn distinguishes between "intellectual" and scientist. C. P. Snow has recently attracted international attention by his description of the Two Cultures—the scientific and the literary. There is no reason why both types of discourse should not continue to exist and develop provided they are not confused. Most people will probably have no difficulty in distinguishing the relatively polemic papers from the empirical and scientific papers mentioned here or elsewhere. Likewise, those who profess to find incongruity in my dabbling in both kinds of writing may profitably survey, from this point of view, the contents of scientific journals.

It was, I suppose, to be expected that most of my polemic writing should be done during the period 1942-1953, and that the subject would be principally international relations and wars. In the 1920's and 1930's I had followed with great interest the debunking of World War I at the hands of Harry Elmer Barnes and S. B. Fay. I do not know how widely my views on international relations were held by other sociologsts. I know for sure that mine were not unanimously approved. At the same time, it may not be entirely irrelevant in this connection to mention that I was in 1942 elected president of the American Sociological Association by the first general election ever to be held by secret ballot. (Up to this time officers of the society had been elected by a voice vote of the members present at the annual meeting.) However, I am compelled to report also that my presidential address to the society on "Sociologists and the Peace" was interrupted with some hisses and boos—not a usual recognition at this annual ceremonial occasion. I do not recall having encountered it before as an accolade to the president of a learned society in my attendance at thirty consecutive meetings of the then Society and now Association.

It appears that I had incurred the displeasure of some of the defenders of certain groups outside sociology. There were also some complaints from within the sociological profession. One member was moved to write the *ASR* objecting to my presidential address, but on patriotic, rather than politico-economic grounds.

The address was not an immortal masterpiece, either as a specimen of academic discourse or as a sample of oratory. Then and now I recognize the full sincerity of those who held views contrary to mine. I do not encourage you to seek out and dust off the February, 1944, *ASR* in which it is printed. However, when I did recently, I confess I was not distressed, even though I have over the passing years grown to recognize more fully the tremendous complexity of the problems involved.

Polemic writing, whether on war and peace or on science, can be illuminating and valuable if it is not taken as a substitute for scientific demonstration.

The next generation of sociologists will have plenty of war and peace to be concerned about, but they are also more skilled in the ways and knowledge of science. Let's see what happens. I've placed my bets.

An Assessment of Lundberg's Substantive Inquiries

WILLIAM R. CATTON, JR.
University of Washington

George Lundberg's earliest papers were almost all concerned with substantive topics, rather than with the positivist stance on meta-sociological issues he later came to symbolize. He wrote on "Sex Differences on Social Questions," "The Newspaper and Public Opinion," "The Demographic and Economic Basis of Political Radicalism and Conservatism," "Campaign Expenditures and Election Results," "The Contents of Radio Programs," and "The Biology of Population Cycles" during his first five years of scholarly output.[1] Even in some of these papers, and with increasing emphasis in some of his later substantive inquiries, his concern with metasociological questions was evident as he dealt with sociological problems.

Some of the titles just quoted belie the image of George Lundberg as a radically physicalistic thinker. Biological, and especially

[1] George A. Lundberg, "Sex Differences on Social Questions," *School and Society,* 23 (May 8, 1926), pp. 595-600; "The Newspaper and Public Opinion," *Social Forces,* 4 (June, 1926), pp. 709-715; "The Demographic and Economic Basis of Political Radicalism and Conservatism," *American Journal of Sociology,* 32 (March, 1927), pp. 719-732; "Campaign Expenditures and Election Results," *Social Forces,* 6 (March, 1928), pp. 452-457; "The Contents of Radio Programs," *Social Forces,* 7 (Sept., 1928), pp. 58-68; "The Biology of Population Cycles," *Social Forces,* 9 (March, 1931), pp. 401-408.

ecological models always interested him, and were implicated in his substantive inquiries.[2] Many people have forgotten or never realized that he decried "absurd attempts to apply the concepts, measures, and terminology of physics and chemistry to social phenomena" on the grounds that such efforts have merely exemplified the common inability of many sociologists to distinguish between the logic of science and the subject-matter of some particular scientific discipline.[3] But when insights into previously unexplained phenomena could be gained by acknowledging parallels between the events studied in one science and those under the purview of another, he saw no point in refusing to pursue the points of similarity. In spite of his interest in organic and ecological models he was imagined by some critics to be wholly a "mechanicist" and opposed to "organicism."[4] This image arose, probably, from his espousal of force-field models, but the image is too narrow to fit the kind of language in which he stated in 1934 some of the conclusions to his two-year study at Columbia University of the leisure patterns of Westchester County. He wrote:

> ... we confront an age when working for the means of livelihood, which has for a million years been the principal preoccupation of the mind and body of man, is about to be relegated to a minor charge upon his time and activity; in its place we have leisure.
>
> The emergence of the new leisure constitutes a major disturbance of the equilibrium of the organism with its environment. When such disturbance occurs the organism engages in restless and craving activity until it achieves a new integration in relation to its surroundings. In the course of such adjustments man has invented many new and strange activities to occupy the time formerly consumed by work for the physical necessities. The description of many of these

[2] See, for example, George A. Lundberg, "Human Social Problems as a Type of Disequilibrium in a Biological Integration," *American Sociological Review*, 6, (Dec., 1948), pp. 689-699; see also George A. Lundberg, *Foundations of Sociology*, New York: Macmillan, 1939, Chapters 5 and 6.

[3] George A. Lundberg, "The Logic of Sociology and Social Research," Chapter 10 in George A. Lundberg, Read Bain, and Nels Anderson (eds.), *Trends in American Sociology*, New York: Harper & Bros., 1929, p. 394.

[4] See, for example, Werner Stark, *The Fundamental Forms of Social Thought*, New York: Fordham University Press, 1963, pp. 151-154.

activities in their various relations occupies the greater part of this volume.[5]

In this Westchester County project, Lundberg and his associates were departing from the conventional paths of substantive sociological interest. As David Quentin Voigt pointed out as recently as 1966 in his book on *American Baseball,* "Even now serious students of leisure carry welts from a 'backlash' of snobbery, laid on by the 'more serious scholars,' who look upon leisure studies as frivolous."[6] Lundberg sought to justify the study of leisure not only by citing its depression-born social urgency, but by pointing out that social science has to be devoted to studying human group behavior, which happens to include play, recreation, artistic and other leisure pursuits. Thus these are at any time proper topics for scientific study, just as any other aspects of human activity.[7]

The volume on the Westchester County study began with a description of the growth of leisure in the modern world, the social problems it potentially poses, and the cultural reasons for its having received little previous study. This introduction was followed with an essentially ethnographic description of the suburban social environment. Quantitative data on the amount, distribution, and uses of leisure were presented, indicating time-expenditure patterns. The multiplicity of voluntary associations in the community pertinent to leisure activity were described. Then an analysis of the suburban family was given, with a description of the impact of family patterns on leisure activity, and vice versa. This was followed by a chapter on the changing role of the church as a leisure outlet. The suburban school was described in a chapter which analyzed the obsolescent aspects of its curriculum and provided an even more extensive analysis of the extracurricular activities that engaged its students. The arts in Westchester were then surveyed, including musical, graphic, and dramatic participation

[5] George A. Lundberg, Mirra Komarovsky, and Mary Alice McInerny, *Leisure: A Suburban Study,* New York: Columbia University Press, 1934, p. 363.

[6] David Quentin Voigt, *American Baseball,* Norman Okla.: University of Oklahoma Press, 1966, p. xi.

[7] *Leisure,* pp. 10-11.

by residents, plus the passive reception of such art forms as radio, motion pictures, and the fine arts. Developments in adult education were reviewed, with an attempt made to separate the vocational aspects from the strictly recreational aspects. Conditions tending to make leisure a community problem were summarized along with reasons for lag in public provision for leisure. Arguments were presented for expansion of government's role in providing facilities and programs for leisure. The concluding chapter made it evident that the broad picture obtained from studying this one suburban county was meant to be generalized to the national society and culture. A methodological note was appended, acknowledging unavoidable sampling deficiencies, and pointing out the serious need for tentativity with respect to many of the descriptive generalizations and conclusions.

Occasional digressions in the Westchester County book seemed to indicate Lundberg's intensifying interest in metasociological matters. Bits of the methodological wisdom he had already compiled in his 1929 volume, *Social Research*,[8] were reasserted here when the substantive topic afforded an excuse. For example, he noted the problems inherent in securing voluntary cooperation from assorted citizens little interested in scholarly research, whose memories and reporting of their own behavior might be highly fallible, and he acknowledged the compounding of these difficulties by serious definitional problems. Lundberg then pointed out that "these difficulties are no greater in a statistical study such as we have here attempted than they are in the voluminous nonstatistical discussions of the same subject. The difficulties only seem less in the latter because rigid definitions of activities and units of time can be largely avoided."[9]

Bearing in mind that this work was done at the onset of the Great Depression when American sociology was incompletely committed to the tradition of questionnaire and interview surveys as a typical research procedure, it is not surprising to find

[8] George A. Lundberg, *Social Research*, New York: Longmans, Green, 1929.
[9] *Leisure*, pp. 88-89.

many pages that sound almost like ethnographic reports. Lundberg wrote that in Westchester County "The chief commercial recreation facilities consist of fifty-four modest movie theaters, and some sixty inns, lodges, hotels, and restaurants which definitely aim to provide leisure diversions as well as food. Only a half a dozen of these are regular hotels; fifteen of them maintain dance facilities; half a dozen are summer hotels providing golf, tennis, swimming, and other diversions; the remainder are inns and restaurants which aim at 'atmosphere,' which is attempted in various ways. Some capitalize their physical surroundings; others their architecture, furnishings and equipment, especially the antique, historic, or foreign touches; still others make much of autographed pictures of the great and near great, especially of actors, musicians, and other artists."[10]

In this same descriptive vein, two full pages were devoted to reproducing a newspaper account of the parade, speeches, and other festivities on Flag Day.[11] But the kinds of data that were beginning to become conventional were also there in profusion: a frequency distribution of the activities of several kinds that occupied 6800 persons while commuting by train into and out of the city;[12] responses of PTA members to questions about what forms of recreation they felt were lacking, what they would do with an additional $1,000 per year, or what they would do with two extra hours of time per day;[13] the detailed diaries some 2400 persons were persuaded to keep of their activities for periods ranging from one to seven days;[14] the responses of high school students to a questionnaire asking for a brief account of the most enjoyable occasion within the past year they could recall. The questionnaire sought data on the time, place, companions, and activities involved in these memorable occasions, and the students' own ideas of why they were so much enjoyed.[15]

[10] *Ibid.*, p. 75.
[11] *Ibid.*, pp. 72-74.
[12] *Ibid.*, p. 46.
[13] *Ibid.*, p. 83.
[14] *Ibid.*, p. 89.
[15] *Ibid.*, pp. 111-112.

Some of the descriptions and comments in the book are as timely today as then. For example: "Unsanitary conditions, impure food and water, polluted air, and nerve-wracking noise are conditions of existence in a modern city against which private personal wealth is largely helpless."[16] Or Lundberg's wry description of the movies available in Westchester theaters sounds much like today's television. Compared with movies exhibited 20 years before the study, plot themes were much the same. His description went like this:

> The stage coach is still being held up by a band of ruffians in the employ of the local saloon-keeper and loan shark. The latter still threatens foreclosure on the ranch of the heroine's father, unless the said heroine agrees to marry the said loan-shark or his ill-favored and wicked son. Nor does the two-gun hero fail to appear at the critical moment when this infamous deal is about to be consummated. After a magnificent ride through canyons and cactus and a prodigious pistol battle with the entire robber band (prolonged applause from the audience), the fade-out still finds him riding down the canyon toward the old homestead with the heroine. Except for the sound equipment and the newsreel, a modern Rip Van Winkle might have fallen asleep twenty years ago in this theater rather than among the hills a few miles away, and awakened to continue the show without suspecting any lapse of time.[17]

Shades of the Ponderosa, or Dodge City.

If the book contained some unacknowledged value-judgments and if its explicit conclusions seemed weak and not very sociologically profound, it nevertheless included some clear and incisive anticipations of the findings of later, more specialized and highly regarded studies. For example, Lundberg pointed out indications which have been corroborated since by several sociologists of religion that the suburban church was then undergoing a secularization process that seemed to be submerging its primary concern with sacraments and worship. He saw it becoming an organization devoted increasingly to providing its members with recrea-

[16] *Ibid.*, p. 349.
[17] *Ibid.*, p. 290.

tional activities.[18] Or, still more pertinent, he described the greater commitment of high school students to their extracurricular preoccupations than to their academic pursuits, in clear and even somewhat detailed anticipation of the more recent studies of the adolescent society.[19]

In the mid-thirties Lundberg turned to consideration of "the Thoughtways of Contemporary Sociology" and such questions as "Is Sociology too Scientific?"—which, of course, he answered in the negative.[20] He also conducted research studies in which he seemed almost as concerned to demonstrate the feasibility of quantification and the usability of such measurement techniques or devices as the Chapin scale and sociograms as he was to produce substantive findings. Both of these devices were involved in his study with Mary Steele of "Social Attraction Patterns in a Village" in Vermont. But this study also was explicitly concerned with hypothesis testing. The leisure study, like much of the work by sociologists in that era, had formulated a few generalizable conclusions after compiling a lot of miscellaneous data, rather than explicitly stating in advance a list of logically interrelated hypotheses to be tested against deliberately marshalled observations. The Lundberg-Steele Vermont village study found support for the following kinds of propositions about the sociometric structure of the community: (1) Choices tended to cluster in socioeconomic classes near to that of the chooser, but were somewhat skewed upward. (2) Sociometric choices were somewhat influenced by, but were hardly dominated by, kinship. (3) Common church membership was one of the clearest factors associated with sociometric choice.[21]

[18] *Ibid.*, p. 217; Cf. J. Milton Yinger, *Religion, Society, and the Individual,* New York: Macmillan, 1957, pp. 293-294, and Thomas Ford Hoult, *The Sociology of Religion,* New York: Dryden, 1958, p.165.

[19] *Leisure,* p. 239; Cf. James S. Coleman, *The Adolescent Society,* New York: Free Press, 1961.

[20] George A. Lundberg, "The Thoughtways of Contemporary Sociology," *American Sociological Review,* 1 (October, 1936), pp. 703-723, and "Is Sociology Too Scientific?" *Sociologus* (Sept., 1933), pp. 298-322.

[21] George A. Lundberg and Mary Steele, "Social Attraction-Patterns in a Village," *Sociometry,* 1 (January-April, 1938), pp. 375-419.

In the leisure study, Lundberg had said that to assert final criteria of human well-being and social desirability would hardly be scientific, but that it was perfectly possible scientifically to determine the scale of values that exists in a community.[22] A scale of values was implied by the village study results. Some years later, after he came to Washington, Lundberg offered specific proposals for the study of human values.[23] But critics continued to accuse him of advocating a sociology that would "neglect" this indispensable concept. For some, this accusation gained plausibility from his perennial insistence that no science tells us what to do with the knowledge it creates, nor is it the business of science to tell us what we should want.[24] Lundberg insisted that value judgments are not scientific conclusions, but he never said they couldn't be data.

What bothered Lundberg most in his later years was the apparent superficiality of the commitment of so many social scientists to the thoughtways of science. He lamented that "having divested ourselves of a few individual examples of our Sunday school superstitions, many of us feel very much liberated, sophisticated, and "scientific" only to fall back so easily in times of crisis "into the familiar personalistic-dramatic pattern of theology in which the forces of Good and Evil under their respective personal leaders again struggle for mastery."[25] These concerns made him receptive to the writings of the revisionist historians after World War II, and he contributed to such literature himself.[26] He wrote for *The*

[22] *Leisure,* p. 22.

[23] George A. Lundberg, "Human Values—A Research Program," *Research Studies of The State College of Washington,* 18 (Sept., 1950), pp. 103-111.

[24] George A. Lundberg, "The Future of the Social Sciences," *Scientific Monthly,* 53 (October, 1941), p. 353.

[25] George A. Lundberg, "Societal Pathology and Sociometry," *Sociometry,* 4 (Feb., 1941), p. 93.

[26] See his reviews of the following books: *"Japanese in the United States? Final Report, Japanese Evacuation from the West Coast,* 1942, in *American Sociological Review,* 9 (Dec., 1944), pp. 713-714; George Morgenstern, *Pearl Harbor: The Study of the Secret War,* in *Social Forces,* 26 (May, 1948), pp. 469-471; Charles A. Beard, *President Roosevelt and the Coming of the War,* 1941, in *The Progressive* (May, 1948); Basil Rauch, *Roosevelt: from Munich to Pearl Harbor,* in the *Chicago Sunday Tribune* (April 16, 1950), Part 4, p. 6; Charles Callen Tansill, *Back Door to War: Roosevelt Foreign Policy,* 1933-1941, in *Social Forces,*

Humanist an essay on "How to Live with People Who Are Wrong," which he also inserted as a final chapter in the second edition of his book *Can Science Save Us?*[27]

Such iconoclastic views were ill-received in wartime when he expressed them pungently in his 1943 presidential address.[28] For these views, and for having the temerity to argue that however understandable it might be, and whatever caused it, Jewish hostility to the Nazi German government nevertheless had to be recognized as an aggravating cause of the German government's hostility toward Jews, Lundberg was accused of having "anti-Semitic" and "pro-facist" attitudes. This orientation was alleged to be the product of his sociological positivism.[29] If fascism means government by a self-appointed elite who suppress all expressions of opposition, the accusation was clearly contradicted by Lundberg's life-long insistence on the importance of distinguishing the role of scientist from the role of citizen, and giving the scientist-citizen no more voice in public policy than might be assented to by other citizens.[30] No sociological writer has been more adamantly opposed to a scientocracy.

There is some indication, however, that the accusation of anti-Semitism influenced Lundberg's subsequent choice of research problems. In response to this accusation, his pre-eminent commitment to the analytic and applied distinction between the scientist's and the citizen's roles came to express itself in a different way. In his wartime presidential address he had argued that legalistic and

---

31 (March, 1953), pp. 297-298. See also his chapter on "American Foreign Policy in the Light of National Interest at Mid-Century," in Harry Elmer Barnes (ed.), *Perpetual War for Perpetual Peace,* Caldwell, Idaho: Caxton, 1953, pp. 555-623.

[27] George A. Lundberg, *Can Science Save Us?* (2nd ed.), New York: Longmans, Green, 1961, Chapter 6.

[28] George A. Lundberg, "Sociologists and the Peace," *American Sociological Review,* 9 (Feb., 1944), pp. 1-13.

[29] Frank E. Hartung, "Sociology of Positivism: Protofascist Aspects," *Science and Society,* 8 (Fall, 1944), pp. 340-341.

[30] George A. Lundberg, "Applying the Scientific Method to Social Phenomena," *Sociology and Social Research,* 34 (Sept.-Oct., 1949), p. 10. The charge of fascist leanings is also contradicted by his years of membership in the American Civil Liberties Union.

moralistic assumptions obstruct sociological research; he had tried to illustrate this point by reference to "large numbers of organized and articulate Jews" who "demand legislation prohibiting criticism ... instead of reckoning with the causes of antagonism."[31] The hostile response he encountered seems to have reinforced his interest in inquiring into "the causes of antagonism." Though he had studied patterns of status differentiation and preferential association before the war (both in Westchester and the Vermont village), he had not done previous research on minority groups as such, nor on ethnocentrism and its consequences. He turned to these topics in the postwar years, as if to substantiate his contention that moralistic and legalistic biases had until then interfered with sound research on these matters by other social scientists. His papers on "Attraction Patterns in a University" and "Selective Association Among Ethnic Groups" came out of this interest, and touched off more controversy.[32]

In Lundberg's own eyes, his pursuit of these research interests was a continuing expression of his persistent conviction that social action programs are more likely to achieve unintended and undesired results when not guided by confirmed scientific knowledge. His aim was to remind social scientists of their duty to leave no obvious stones unturned in their search for causes and correlates of any phenomenon they sought to explain. If his substantive conclusions seem to his critics to reflect his preconceptions, the remedy obviously consists in further research. Preconceptions need to be tested, not just pointed out and assailed.

George Lundberg invested his academic career in vigorous and influential advocacy of the method of natural science for the pursuit of sociological knowledge. For several decades he stood out as a symbol in the minds of friends and opponents of so-called neopositivism. A large part of his writing was devoted to stating and clarifying the postulates of scientific thought, the fundamental

[31] "Sociologists and the Peace," p. 3.

[32] George A. Lundberg, Virginia Beasley, and Lenore Dickson, "Attraction Patterns in a University," *Sociometry,* 12 (Feb.-Aug., 1949); George A. Lundberg and Lenore Dickson, "Selective Association Among Ethnic Groups," *American Sociological Review,* 17 (Feb., 1952), pp. 23-35.

traits of objective research, and the applicability of such principles to sociological inquiry. He insisted that there are no characteristics of social phenomena and no feature of scientific method that would preclude the rigorous adherence to that method in the investigation of those phenomena.[33]

He gave particular emphasis to two major implications of this position: First, he argued adamantly that quantification of sociological concepts is possible and should be pursued diligently even though on the frontiers of the discipline there would always be subjective elements, speculative propositions, and qualitative procedures. In his own research on substantive topics, he tried to be as consistently quantitative in his approach as the techniques and tools of the time and his training permitted. In the era of computerized research, of course, Lundberg's achievement of quantification in his own studies will come to seem less and less impressive, just as Lindbergh's daring transatlantic flight has lost its power to thrill the youngsters of today who aspire to be astronauts. Second, he consistently stressed that the achievement of scientific competence required sociologists in their scientific role to abandon their traditional ethical and moralistic orientations toward subject-matter. It is not the business of science to praise or blame, and doing so impedes the achievement of accurate description, reliable prediction, and valid explanation. Again, the fact that obvious value-judgments can be found among his ostensibly factual research conclusions may mislead us if we compare his writing with the output of those he influenced rather than comparing both with the output of his predecessors and his contemporaries.

[33] "The Logic of Sociology and Social Research," pp. 403-404.

Comments on Lundberg's Sociological Theories

FRANZ ADLER
California State College, Los Angeles

George Andrew Lundberg's greatness, his claim to a permanent place in the annals of the science of sociology, lies in his relentless insistence upon empirical research, empirical verification of theory, and on empirical relevance of every sentence, of every word said in a sociological context. It lies in his insistence on quantification.[1] This is merit enough and if the sociological theory he developed does not fully satisfy us, instead of blaming a truly great and good man for this shortcoming we should try to discover the factors which impeded his achieving perfection in the area of theory. This may teach us to avoid these same pitfalls and to help George Lundberg to achieve the goal which is common to all members of the scientific community. As Max Weber put it: "Scientific work is chained to the course of progress . . . each of us knows that what he has accomplished will be antiquated in ten, twenty, fifty years. This is the fate to which science is subjected; it is the very meaning of scientific work . . ."[2]

[1] The author is indebted to an unpublished paper by his friend and colleague John Munns which discusses relations between Lundberg's philosophy and his sociology.

[2] Max Weber, "Science as a Vocation," in Hans H. Gerth and C. Wright Mills, translators and editors, *From Max Weber: Essays in Sociology*, New York, Oxford University Press, 1946, pp. 137-138.

Lundberg's theory was fully presented in his *Foundations of Sociology* in 1939.[3] After that he occasionally discussed specific matters in various contexts, but he did not leave us another systematic presentation of his theoretical views. A paperback published under the same title of *Foundations of Sociology* in 1964 omits the Chapters V to XIII of the earlier work which deal with substantive theory and is restricted to his metasociological thoughts.[4] Three editions of his introductory text,[5] considerably differing from each other and undoubtedly incorporating changes in his maturing opinions, cannot be used fairly as bases for the discussion of his own thinking as they were written in cooperation with others. No matter how great the affinity among the views of collaborators on any publication, not even they themselves can always be sure at a later time which passages were written with unanimity, which ones as the results of compromise, and which ones with a resigned shrug of the shoulders of one or several among them.

This consideration seems to be even more than usually appropriate in the case of an author who had an urge to present his views as being in agreement with those of others and who seemed to derive great satisfaction from the observation of "convergences".[6] In this point he seems to exhibit a faith strangely similar to that of the early Parsons who managed to derive proof of the fact that his views were correct from recognizing his own work as a synthesis or "convergence" of varying and dialectically diverging intellectual streams or currents.[7]

In his basic philosophic outlook Lundberg tried to synthesize pragmatism and positivism. Or perhaps, he merely did not notice the difference. This may again be attributable to a lack of fluency

[3] New York, The Macmillan Company, 1939.

[4] New York, David McKay Co., Inc., 1964.

[5] George A. Lundberg, Clarence C. Schrag, Otto N. Larsen, *Sociology,* New York, Harper & Brothers, 1954, revised edition, 1958, third edition, 1963.

[6] George A. Lundberg, "Methodological Convergences between Mead, Lundberg, and Parsons," *American Journal of Sociology,* vol. LX, 1954, pp. 182-184; "Epilogue," in *Foundations of Sociology,* 1964, pp. 161-170.

[7] Talcott Parsons, *The Structure of Social Action,* New York, McGraw-Hill Book Co., Inc., 1937, pp. 10-12, pp. 722 ff; see also Pitirim A. Sorokin, *Sociological Theories of Today,* New York, Harper & Row, Publishers, 1966, pp. 404-405.

in foreign languages which prevented him from reading then untranslated materials from foreign authors both in the philosophy of science and in sociology proper. When more complete translations of works of the Vienna Circle philosophers and of Max Weber became available in English, pressures of research, teaching and administration undoubtedly had become too heavy for him to permit a complete rethinking of earlier pronouncements.[8]

Had he been more fully familiar with Max Weber, Dilthey, Rickert and other members of the German *Verstehen* school, he might have been more reluctant in accepting so wholeheartedly the teachings of George Herbert Mead. It is hard to comprehend how a supposedly radical empiricist aiming at predictability in human behavior could say without any reservations whatsoever, "I have never had occasion to differ with George Herbert Mead . . . ,"[9] and swallow whole the concept of a by definition unobservable "I" considered as a source of arbitrary choices and essential human unpredictability. Such a concept may be "useful" in the pragmatists' sense as an ideological crutch to a faith in the freedom of the will,[10] but it has absolutely no business in a natural science of sociology as Lundberg certainly wanted to develop it. Of course, in those days, it was "the mode to be a Meadian" as Read Bain put it so well at the Cleveland meetings of the American Sociological Society.

Lundberg rejected the view that explanation of social phenomena must consist in their reduction to psychological phenomena[11] and suggested that "conceptualized description" constitutes "the only explanation known in science."[12] But a few lines later he says ". . . anything is 'explained' or 'understood' when we have reduced a situation to elements and correlations *with which we are so familiar that we accept them as a matter of course* . . ." Apparently he did not realize that this common sense notion of satisfied curiosity is inconsistent with the scientific meaning of explanation.

[8] See, however, George A. Lundberg, "The Natural Science Trend in Sociology," *American Journal of Sociology,* vol. LXI, November, 1955, pp. 191-202.

[9] "Methodological Convergences between Mead, Lundberg, and Parsons," *American Journal of Sociology,* Vol. LX, 1954, p. 183.

[10] *Foundations,* 1939, p. 128, footnote 7.

[11] *Ibid.,* p. 120, footnote 7.

[12] *Ibid.,* p. 6.

He knew this scientific meaning and stated it well: "Thus are . . . events . . . explained by showing that they are only special cases of a general rule or law" already known.[13] The man on the street, the run of the mill sociologist, and—unfortunately—others say they "understand" social phenomena when they have reduced them to what they think is psychology. And—unfortunately—Lundberg accepted Mead while—in keeping with his stated philosophies—the only psychology he should have accepted and used, if any at all, is that of behaviorism.

The acceptance of Mead's philosophy on the one hand and an interest in the writings of the semanticists on the other lead to his participating in that overemphasis on symbols which still leads to so much confusion in contemporary strivings toward a scientific sociology. It leads him to restricting the social interaction concept to symbolic interaction, thus unnecessarily excluding any other.[14] Due to the widespread belief—unproved and without any possibility of proof—that symbolic behavior is a human monopoly absolutely unknown and unavailable to other animals, this definition precluded and delayed—perhaps for ever—the use of animal experiments in Sociology.[15] No reminder is needed as to how much such experiments have contributed to the extent to which scientific psychology has overtaken scientific sociology. Further, using the "symbol" concept, Lundberg on the one hand emphasised that words were just words and nothing but words. On the other hand, he asserted, that words or "symbols . . . are the data of sociological science."[16]

This I consider a serious error. Words, pictures, signs, graphs, and numbers are indeed symbols and they are the inexpendable and unavoidable tools of scientific reasoning (as of all or nearly all forms of reasoning), but these symbols are the data of specific sciences as, for example, linguistics, mathematics, iconography, etc.

[13] *Ibid.*, pp. 253-256.

[14] ". . . . interaction among human beings is recognized as being at least in one respect highly unique. It is unique. It is unique in that it takes place by means of mechanisms of *communication through symbolic behavior*." *Ibid.*, p. 253.

[15] See, for example, *Ibid*, 1939, p. 278.

[16] *Ibid.*, p. 121.

This is the case because they are the phenomena these sciences deal with. Sociology, however, deals with all social phenomena and with symbols only to the extent as they are part of these social phenomena. The process of symbolization—and let us remember that there are many varied ways of symbolizing the same phenomena—may be studied by psychologists, logicians, philosophers of science, and methodologists, but not by sociologists. The latter, like all other scientists, aim at the study of observable events as their data, not at the study of symbols used in conceptualizing and representing them. Contrary to Lundberg and to the pragmatists, responses are not what is known, but they are the means of knowing. What we try to symbolize is not the response, but whatever it may be that has been responded to. While it may not be possible to prove the real existence of this or any other part of the outside world to the philosophers' satisfaction, the denial of its reality will lead to freeway accidents, to lots of other trouble, and finally to the psychiatrist's couch. Sociology, like any other science, must avoid the cloud-cuckoo land of individual and collective hallucination. It must produce concepts (symbols) that stand in such a relation to the external world that they enable us to manipulate it so that our responses to it become more pleasurable and less painful. Events, rather than responses to events, must be the data of sociology. Symbols are not the data, they are representations of data, they are not given, but they are elaborated from the given or imposed upon it. Data are stubborn, unyielding, final. Symbols are provisional, always liable to be discarded in favor of others better suited to the scientific task at hand. Lundberg realized this in his critique of the "mere word" but he failed to draw the necessary conclusion from this insight when he designated symbols as the subject matter of sociology. If there are no "things in nature to correspond to words in (our) vocabulary"[17] we are not talking science but phantasy. Symbolization is part of interpretation and the scienctific observer must learn to separate interpretation from observation, at least to reduce their fusion to an absolutely unavoidable minimum, or he will never rise out of the morass of common sense.

[17] *Ibid.*, p. 278.

Lundberg criticized the error of mistaking the symbol for the referent (which he well knew is the real object of science)[18] and his emphasis on this separation is one of his most important contributions to sound sociological thinking. But he also tried to attach the symbol firmly to the observational data it is intended to refer to. As a means of achieving the connection between the symbol and its referents he suggested the use of "operational definitions",[19] that is definitions which explain a term by indicating the way of measuring or producing it's referent. The former (definition by method of measurement) is uniquely suited to the present state of physics as a science. If a letter of the alphabet or any other symbol occurs in a mathematical formula, this formula can be expected to yield correct results only if and when numbers to be substituted for this symbol are arrived at in a specified way. Furthermore, the metric system of physics is a set of statements about basic relationships in the observable universe. They indicate transmutation ratios for length, volume, time, as well as sound, heat, electric currents, and other forms of energy in all their manifestations. Consequently, in physics a definition in terms of a method of measurement immediately locates the definiendum in relation to all the major classes of phenomena. The measurements of sociology, on the other hand, still remain isolated from each other, woefully unrelated among and intransmutable into each other. Thus little or nothing is gained by defining our terms operationally except in the clarification of quantitative statements. At the present stage of our measurement techniques our search for theory is not advanced by relying on definitions of this kind.[20] We may, however, advance in this direction by striving to define all our concepts in terms of some kind of basic units.

[18] *Ibid.*, p. 243.

[19] *Ibid.*, p. 26, pp. 151-152.

[20] cf. Franz Adler, "Operationism," in Julius Gould and William L. Kolb, *A Dictionary of the Social Sciences*, New York, The Free Press of Glencoe, 1964, pp. 475-477; Lundberg himself defined very few of his concepts "operationally", in fact, he even rejects such a definition (justly indeed) in at least one case: "Correlation is not merely the name of a certain statistical operation invented by Karl Pearson. It is, as the dictionary says, . . .," *Foundations*, 1939, p. 52.

Timasheff has suggested that one of the basic requirements of any sociological theory is that it designates what is to be considered as the unit in the system.[21] Lundberg's discussion would lead the reader to expect the unit to be one of adjustment, energy, force, behavior, or interaction. Adjustment, "the situation under which the activities of an organism come to rest or equilibrium,"[22] may be a zero point of reference, but there is no indication how it is to be distinguished from death nor is a uniform method indicated for measuring equilibrium or *dis*equilibrium which would yield units for a system. "Energy" is observed as "energy transformation" which in turn appears as "movement (behavior)." "Energy. . .is the change from one type of (relatively stable electron—proton) symmetry to another." "Energy" also is ". . .a name for amounts of changes in relationships." Finally, it is *"force times amount of change* in some societal characteristic."[23] The last definition does implicitly designate a unit. No unit of either energy or energy transformation is offered, however, which need not be calculated with the help of some more basic unit. Furthermore, there is no suggestion as to how this "energy" can be observed other than in the behavior embodying it, which leads to the conclusion that we have here primarily a fancy name replacing the common and everyday name "behavior". "Force" is defined as the rate of changes in relationships in time. Lundberg also accepts Dodd's definition of force: "a time rate of change ('velocity') times a population, divided by time to get the rate of change of velocity (which is 'acceleration').[24] Lundberg's and Dodd's definitions seem to differ, but neither is designed as an independent variable or a basic unit. They rather point to force as a function of or another name for changes in other units. Lundberg suggests that formulas describing energy phenomena in other sciences may have some analogous

[21] Nicholas S. Timasheff, *Sociological Theory, its Nature and Growth,* revised edition, New York, Random House, 1963, p. 11.

[22] *Foundations,* 1939, p. 5; for a discussion of the ambiguity of the "equilibrium" concept see William R. Catton, Jr., *From Animistic to Naturalistic Sociology,* New York, McGraw-Hill Book Company, 1966, p. 15.

[23] *Foundations,* 1939, pp. 203, 204, and 206, and, quoting Stuart C. Dodd, 236.

[24] *Ibid.,* pp. 205 and 236; cf. Pitirim A. Sorokin, Review of *Foundations of Sociology, American Journal of Sociology,* XLV, 1939-40, pp. 795-798.

uses in sociology. This suggestion which has shown itself fruitful in some research undertakings does not really warrant the big metaphysical treatment given to it in the *Foundations.* While we *may* wish to suggest "greater unity underlying widely disparate phenomena," we do *not "must* assume (this) as a hypothesis."[25] We may wish to wait for the data to lead us to take this step.

It is in regard to behavior that Lundberg approaches most closely the conceptualization of a theoretical unit. Had he known Max Weber's little set of basic definitions in terms of social actions and probabilities,[26] he might have decided to adapt Weber's definitional method to a more radically empirical sociology. As it is, he left this opportunity to me for which I shall always be grateful to him.[27] I also gratefully acknowledge his leadership by just quoting two of his statements from the *Foundations*: "These movements (behaviors) of man which determine his status (relationships) in a group are the general concern of the social sciences", and "the distinctively social basis for classification is *interaction,* and strictly speaking, this should be the sole basis of *sociological* classification."[28]

Four concepts taken from A. F. Bentley[29] and quoted by Lundberg might have served as unit concepts: the "dicaud," a verbal behavioral interpersonal event and the "dicaudane", "this wider event, which includes not merely the speaker, hearer, and air, but also the embodied reference." These concepts are expanded into the more general "communact" which designates "the general case of men seen in communication in that specialized observation which provisionally defers examination of the 'what' that the communication is about," and the "communicane," "the general case of instances of communication, in which men are seen in 'com-

[25] *Foundations,* 1939, p. 207.

[26] Max Weber, *Basic Concepts in Sociology,* Translated by H. P. Secher, New York, Philosophical Library, 1962; Max Weber, *The Theory of Social and Economic Organization,* translated by Henderson and Parsons, New York, The Free Press of Glencoe, Inc., 1947.

[27] Franz Adler, "A Unit Concept for Sociology," *American Journal of Sociology,* LXV, 1960, pp. 356-364.

[28] *Foundations,* 1939, pp. 203 and 360-361.

[29] A. F. Bentley, *Behavior, Knowledge, Fact,* Bloomington, Ind., Principia Press, 1935, pp. 231, 233, 251.

munication about something.' "[30] But, after these units have been mentioned and defined, they do not recur in Lundberg's writings again. They do not even appear in the index of the *Foundations.* Though the terms and their definitions are, perhaps, somewhat clumsy by today's standards, they might have been adapted and put to good use. Of particular interest is the distinction between generalization on a level of content or meaning and generalizaton on a higher level, a level of pure form in Simmel's sense. This distinction may someday come to mark the dividing line between those levels which today, generally with little or no clarification, are referred to as theories of the middle range on the one hand and all encompassing grand theories on the other.

In Chapter IX of his book, Lundberg discusses types of groups under the heading of "Population—P," thus implying, perhaps, that he considered the individual as the basic unit of sociological discourse. But this is not the case.[31] He asserts, quite to the contrary, that the group is equally real and/or unreal as the individual and assures us that it is justifiable to refer to the group as an organism. The group can behave as well and as much as the individual.[32] In the context of arguments current in those days, he emphasized the metaphysical nature of the argument concerning "reality" and fell right into the trap of symbolism and semantics by asserting that all we are talking about are just words, i.e., symbols, and by losing sight of the only question that matters, namely, what *can* we know, what *can* we observe? And I maintain and am willing to swear on a stack of Bibles that whenever I have observed any kind of action it was that of an individual. Sometimes I have been told or was lead by my common sense cultural upbringing to

[30] *Foundations,* 1939, p. 254.

[31] *Ibid.,* pp. 339-374.

[32] *Ibid.,* pp. 162, 164, 165, 166: "We shall speak of the behavior of groups . . . in exactly the same sense as we speak of the behavior of individuals," and 192: "The refined analysis of this (group) behavior . . . is the task that confronts us." See also George A. Lundberg, "Social Problems as a Type of Disequilibrium in a Biological Integration," *American Sociological Review,* Vol. XIII, 1948, pp. 689-699, specifically p. 690: The individual does not possess a "reality not possessed by an interacting group of individuals," same page: ". . . whether human society is or is not an organism is a futile question . . . ."

consider that a specific act of a specific human being was an act of the state, the university, the society, or whatnot. But I never *saw* this to be the case. Neither has any sociologist ever given me a criterion or a method by which I might be able to distinguish generally and with high probability of validation by others the act of a group from the act of an individual. In the legal sphere, of course, the matter has been clarified, but not necessarily in a manner that satisfies all sociological needs. Hans Kelsen, for example, who identifies the state or the corporation with its normative order, states that an individual acts within the framework of that order as an organ of that collective, if he acts in the manner to which the norms of the organization obligate him (and in no other). Then and only then, it is the organization that acts, otherwise it is the individual.[33] This still leaves a lot to be desired. Does the inductee obeying orders to report at the induction station act as an organ of the state, that is, as the state? Is he then, the state reporting to itself at the station? This is enough of a difficulty, but the views of jurisprudence certainly are of no help at all, when groups are concerned to which the legal order does not grant "juristic" or as it is sometimes called, "moral" personality. The crowd, the family, the friendship group, the partnership, etc. cannot act in any mnaner distinguishable by law from that of the individual actually behaving. "Juristic" personality is a fiction, useful for legal purposes. Analogous assumptions in sociology merely confuse the thinking of sociology students and their teachers.

[33] Hans Kelsen, *General Theory of Law and State,* translated by Anders Wedberg, Cambridge, Massachusetts, Harvard University Press, 1949, pp. 97-98: "And indeed acts of a juristic person are always acts of human beings designated as acts of a juristic person. They are acts of those individuals who act as organs of juristic person. Jurisprudence is thus faced with the task of determining when an individual is acting as an organ of a juristic person . . . only the behavior of human beings can be regulated by the legal order, the duties and rights of individual human beings . . .An individual acts as an organ of the corporation if his behavior corresponds in a certain way to the special order which constitutes the corporation . . . The corporation and 'its' statute, the normative order regulating the behavior of some individuals and the association (community) 'constituted' by the order, are not two different entities, they are identical . . . It is therefore misleading to say that an association or a community is 'formed' by or composed of individuals . . . The association or community is made up only of those acts of individuals which are determined by the order . . . The association or community is nothing but 'its' order."

Regardless of the metaphysical reality or unreality of groups, the sociologist as an observer can rid himself of the problem of how to impute a given behavior either to its physiological performer or to one or another group he may belong to. He takes it as the individual's behavior and considers it in terms of situations, roles, previous events, and any other variables connectable to it according to his needs with regard to their usefulness in establishing an empirical, scientific description of what goes on in, with, and around groups.

One of the sources of Lundberg's failure in arriving at a genuine theory of sociology, then, was his philosophic confusion. Another, closely related to it, was his inability to decide upon a unit concept. A third one may be suspected to lie in ideas concerning theory construction current in the thirties and forties with which he agreed most likely. The way I was taught in those days in graduate school over and over again by one eminent professor after another, you started by formulating problems, thought up some likely answers to them as hypotheses, and then went on to test them. When you had tested them thoroughly and had arrived at a valid generalization, *then and only then and not any sooner*, you looked at this generalization in relation to other validated generalizations and then hypothesized toward a higher level of generalization. And only when this higher level generalization was fully tested, *only then* were you permitted to progress by inference from this and other valid generalizations of the same level of abstraction to move up another step in inference. This seemed so obvious and apparently undisputed that it was not even clearly spelled out. Nobody who saw the scientific method according to this model could possibly conceive of proposing any high or even middle level theory.

But there are alternatives open even to the most conscientious proponent of empiricism in sociology.

1. We may build up pyramids of hypothetical generalizations from the lowest to the highest level, not waiting for the verification of any, realizing the increasing uncertainty as we move upward in the degree of generality. This method, while possible in theory, is not likely to be carried out honestly by anybody. While claiming

and, perhaps, even believing, to proceed that way he is probably going to do exactly the opposite:

2. We may start with one or several assumptions of very high level generality and then deduce progressively lower level generalizations from them. This alternative permits the formulation of "theories of the middle range" as well as of "grand theory" provided that even the latter be cast in a terminology which will make it possible to test by observations all lower level generalizations derived from it by deduction. Whether or not such a theory now actually exists is a matter very much argued among sociologists today.

3. The overall theory most satisfactory to the empiricist which is possible at this point in the development of factual knowledge in sociology may be a formal theory in the shape of a mathematical model.[34]

The construction of such a theory must rest on a clear statement of what is considered as knowable. Going somewhat beyond the lead of George Lundberg, I consider as knowable only what I and other statistically normal observers can observe with our senses. This eliminates, at least for the time being, any internal events. The unobservable may well exist quite as really or even more so than the observable. But this particular theory will have to be restricted to that which is observable. Whether or not a theory under this restriction will be as efficient, more efficient, or less efficient in predicting observable events or in explaining them (in the sense that the explanandum could have been predicted from the *explanans*) as one taking other matters into account remains to be seen when the powers of both theories are comparatively tested by observations.

As the unit of this theory I propose the social behavior item, that is the smallest meaningful bit of behavior followed by somebody else's behavior that could have been predicted from it. I wish to define all the terms of sociology in terms of social behavior. Among

[34] cf. for a small scale example, Franz Adler and Herman Loether, "Group Discussions as Persuasion Processes: A Mathematical Model," *Sociologia Internationalis,* IV, 1966, pp. 27-48.

other results I should be enabled thereby to eliminate a very large percentage of the traditionally used terms which turn out to have identical meanings when defined in terms of the same unit. For example, attitudes, interests, personality traits, habits, values, and behavior patterns, all turn out to be behavior probabilities. Another result would be a clear recognition of certain logically necessary relationships between individuals, roles, structures, groups, society and culture.[35]

Social behavior is to be measured by the relative frequency of its occurrence in a given kind of situation, the social behavior probability. Relationships, groups, systems are defined as sets of such probabilities. Processes may be seen as chains of probabilities of social behavior.[36]

The relationships or probabilities of social behavior which are considered as forming a system are conceived as doing this when they in turn are related to each other. In other words, a relationship between A and B consists of the likelihood that when A does a', B does in p_1 percent of the cases b'. At the same time in a relation of C and D, d' tends to follow c' with a probability of p_2. If in time the relationship a':b' becomes p_1', and the relationship c':d' becomes p_2' and so on, and if the changes in p_2 and p_1 appear to be predictable from each other we may say that the relationship between A and B is related to the relationship between C and D.[37]

A system should be regarded as including processes (chains of probabilities of social behavior) as well as relationships which are functionally related to each other. Thus, changes in the chain sequences also may be related to changes in other chain sequences as well as to changes in relationships and changes in relations between relationships.[38]

I believe that today a very simple actually existing system could

[35] Franz Adler, "A Unit Concept for Sociology," *American Journal of Sociology*, LXV, 1960, pp. 356-364.

[36] Adler and Loether, *exp. cit.*

[37] Franz Adler, "Toward a 'Simple' Mathematical Model of Society," *Sociological Inquiry*, Spring, 1967, pp. 211-215.

[38] Franz Adler, "Functionalism Made Verifiable," *Sociological Quarterly*, IV, 1963, pp. 59-70.

be described in this manner with reasonable ease. And, if this is possible in practice, then any system, no matter how large or complex, could be so described in theory. This description would at first merely indicate the mathematical forms of possible relationships and processes, and relations between and among them. Later it would be filled in gradually with concretely observed content.

This is what was meant by the statement much earlier in this paper: highly generalized theory is likely to appear in purely mathematical form at this time. It would present a formal universal basic pattern of all groups, systems, and societies, extant and possible. Then, at any given time, before all relevant knowledge is gathered, including that about all other social beings on this Earth, on all the planets of this solar system, of the galaxy, and of the universe, there will be increasingly general theories of increasingly broader middle ranges and with increasingly concrete contents.

If and when this becomes possible, I hope that we as well as our sociological descendants will always remain gratefully conscious both of the tremendous impulse George Lundberg once gave to sociology toward empiricism and toward quantification as well as of what we have learned from him by going further than he did in the direction toward which he pointed as well as by avoiding his minor mistakes.

George Lundberg's Social Philosophy: A Continuing Dialogue[1]

HARRY ALPERT
University of Oregon and UNESCO

If I were forced by some dictator to summarize George Lundberg's social philosophy in one word, I would select the word SCIENCE. Salvation through science! Yes, science can save us; science as helmsman of life; science as the basis of faith; science as the wave of the future; science as the need of the present; science as the motive force of the past; science, science, and more science. Science here, science there, everywhere science, science, science. In preparation for this presentation I re-read much of what George Lundberg wrote over a thirty-five year span. I was struck by the persistence, insistence, and consistency of the theme. His various writings, empirical, political, philosphical, or methodological, are only variations on the basic theme: Some science is here; more science is coming, and soon, utopia of utopias, all will be science. George Lundberg was, indeed, a super-salesman of science. Did he, as Jessie Bernard once suggested[2], zealously and dangerously oversell his product?

[1] Presented to Pacific Sociological Association, April 1, 1967, at Long Beach, California, as part of a plenary session on "George Lundberg: The Many Roles of a Sociologist." The assistance of the National Science Foundation (Grant No. GS 291) is gratefully acknowledged.

[2] Jessie Bernard, "Reply to Lundberg's Comments," *American Sociological Review,* 14 (December, 1949), p. 799.

In a sense, George Lundberg was a true son of the Enlightenment in his emphasis on the improvement of the human race through science as the highest embodiment of Reason. He was a true son of the Enlightenment, also, in his unreasoning, emotional faith in science and his stoical posture toward the failure of mankind to espouse the cause of science. Consider, for example, the final sentence of the original edition of "Can Science Save Us?": "When we give our undivided faith to science, we shall possess a faith more worthy of allegiance than many we vainly have followed in the past, and we also shall accelerate the translation of our faith into actuality."[3]

For all his posture about behaving scientifically, George Lundberg's charm as a human being (one of the many roles of a sociologist) lay in his total, undivided, almost humorless, highly polemic, extremely emotional, persistent, and stubborn dedication to two fundamental propositions: (1) Science is man's most effective way of achieving mastery over his physical environment, and (2) the methods of science are man's most effective way of achieving mastery over his human relations and social organization. His admiration of the obvious achievements of the physical sciences and his contempt for the equally obvious failures of human social relations provided him with the opportunity of describing, in various contexts, and in colorful language, the ironic contrasts between the two worlds. He wrote, "To be qualified to pull a tooth or remove an appendix, we require people to study systematically for seven or eight years beyond high school. To keep nations from flying at each others' throats, any political hack will do."[4]

Science as do-all and cure-all, or scientism (to give it proper philosophical dignity), is a respectable enough philosophy. Moreover, the doctrine, based on the inclusion of man in nature, that the scientific method can properly be extended to the study of human social behavior is, despite some strong opposition in

[3] George A. Lundberg, *Can Science Save Us?* New York: Longmans, Green and Co., 1947, p. 115.

[4] *Ibid.*, p. 65.

certain quarters, a reasonable proposition. Unfortunately, Lundberg muddied the waters considerably by insisting that his fundamental position be properly described as *Natural Science.*[5] Note the adjective Natural. Adjectives, in general, are frightful impediments to clear thinking. Perhaps it was the polemicist streak in him, but by his shrill insistence on *natural* science, Lundberg committed what I have elsewhere called the fallacy of the misplaced qualifier.[6] Many of us are victims of this fallacy. We say "natural science" or "social science," but the adjectives are not intended as descriptions of science but rather as descriptions of a particular subject-matter of science. Consider, for example, the controversy over Durkheim's conception of sociology as an objective science. In the phrase "objective science," the adjective does not refer to the subject-matter of the science, but to the science itself, that is, to the nature of the body of rules and principles of procedures which we generally call the scientific method. We say that a science is objective when its procedural apparatus includes rules for universal verification and validation, when, in other words, it provides a means by which its empirical results may be accurately and reliably checked by any physically and mentally competent observer who cares to do so.[7]

One must approach, similarly, Lundberg's use of *Natural* Science. Natural science, indeed! What other kind of science is there? Unnatural science? Natural as distinct from what? In his controversy with Paul Furfey, Lundberg seemed to be opposing the natural sciences to the moral sciences.[8] Moral science? Should we, then, think about "immoral science"?

[5] George A. Lundberg, "The Natural Science Trend in Sociology," *American Journal of Sociology,* 61 (November, 1955), p. 191. Lundberg undoubtedly welcomed the title and posture, if not all of the content, of Professor William R. Catton's volume, *From Animistic to Naturalistic Sociology,* New York: McGraw-Hill, 1966.

[6] Harry Alpert, "The Fallacy of the Misplaced Qualifier," *American Sociological Review,* 25 (June, 1960), pp. 406-407.

[7] See Harry Alpert, *Emile Durkheim and His Sociology,* New York: Columbia University Press, 1939, p. 112.

[8] George A. Lundberg, "The Natural Science Trend in Sociology," *American Journal of Sociology,* 61 (November, 1955), pp. 197-199.

The fallacy of the misplaced qualifier is also committed by those who fail to distinguish between a social process and the scientific analysis of that process. Science refers to a way of understanding phenomena, not to the way in which phenomena behave. Gases do not behave scientifically in following Boyle's Law. Boyle behaved scientifically in developing his law of gases. Similarly, the scientific study of, say, foreign policy, does not make the behavior of foreign policy makers scientific. It is illusory to assume that the rational analysis of human behavior necessarily leads people to be more rational in their behavior.

Lundberg was an ardent advocate of the unity of science and insisted that that unity derived from its logical and methodological requirements.[9] What, then, is the significance of the adjective "natural" as applied to science? The use of the phrase "natural science" strikes me as grossly incompatible with the epistemological position adopted by Lundberg, namely that knowledge relates not to the nature of things but to the operations of the knower. If there are "no things in themselves," no inherent "essences," then everything is natural or human, or what have you. The adjective has lost its power to distinguish or differentiate.

Yet, the fact that Lundberg used the phrase "natural science" has philosophical significance. I began to develop the major characteristics of what I wanted to call the Lundberg syndrome and soon realized that the task had already been performed for me, in large measure, by Professor Catton.[10] In a table entitled "Assorted metascientific positions, classified by their apparent relation to naturalism," he presents a left-hand column with the heading, "Tend to be anti-naturalistic" and a right-hand column headed, "Tend to be naturalistic." This latter column includes physicalism, mechanism, positivism, and empiricism. These issues, plus naturalism and operationalism, fairly well sum up the Lundbergian philosophy. I respect Catton's warning not to think of naturalism as meaning any one of these other issues or as meaning all of them in combination. I believe, however, that Lundbergian

[9] *Ibid.*, p. 199.
[10] Catton, *Op. cit.*, p. 27.

scientism may be said to contain strong doses of the issues listed in Catton's right-hand column. There may be symbolic significance in placing these issues on the right, as I shall discuss later.[11]

I began by saying that I could sum up Lundberg's philosophy in one word. Will you permit me a second one? My second word is POLEMIC. Is polemicism a social philosophy or a way of life? Lundberg loved a battle and viewed debate and controversy as avenues to clarity and understanding. Lundberg vs. MacIver, Lundberg vs. Lynd, Lundberg vs. Blumer (no mean polemicist himself), Lundberg vs. Jessie Bernard, Lundberg vs. Paul Furfey, Lundberg vs. the entire American Sociological Society, and finally, later in life, it was Lundberg vs. the Zionists.

Call it stance, style, technique, manner, posture, or pose, one cannot explain or understand George Lundberg without that special operation called the polemic. I never heard him say so, but he must have believed that the Letter to the Editor was an efficacious instrument of philosphical discourse, if not of social change. In fact, many of his journal articles are basically extended letters to the editor.

His love of argumentation was enormous and made him intellectually exciting. George Lundberg's polemicism and argumentativeness led him far afield in his effort to win an argument. He resorted, at times, to an exasperating pun, a twist of words, or a play of language. Even when he was serious, it was difficult not to feel that he was "putting on," as the contemporary expression goes. Consider, for example, his famous, or infamous, debate with Robert MacIver over the similarity of explaining a piece of paper flying in the wind and a man flying from a crowd. In all seriousness, without a smile, or even a suggestion that he is enjoying a play on words, Lundberg concludes the discussion with the grandiose—shall I say pompous?—observation that "the principle of parsimony requires that we seek to bring into the same framework the explanation of all flying objects." Come, come, George! How about the principle of good old common sense? Is it necessary

[11] George A. Lundberg, *Foundations of Sociology,* New York: The Macmillan Co., 1939, p. 13.

to ignore the differences in meaning of the term "flying" to win an argument?

Several years later, Lundberg finally conceded that there may be different ways of studying a flying piece of paper and a fleeing man. Sociology, he wrote in 1955, undoubtedly involves instruments and empirical techniques peculiar to itself, as does every natural science.[12] The "essential" difference, he adds, "from the point of view of causation between the paper flying before the wind and the man before a crowd disappears if in each case *all the influences* of which the 'flying' is the resultant are in each case accounted for by methods subject to corroboration, of the type recognized in the natural sciences. Among these influences, in the case of the man, the natural science sociologist would, as a matter of course, include *all* his mental states, his cultural background, and his appreciation of the significance of the crowd's pursuit, to the extent that they are observable in the scientific sense (a problem of technology). The mental appreciation of significance, if it exists and is an influence in determining the man's flight, exists in the form of language symbols, which the man can communicate to himself and to us and which, therefore, are observable and subject to check. In short, all the influences the 'moral' scientist would seek out, except those which the 'moral' scientist professes to secure through occult and uncheckable processes, are included also by the natural science sociologist."[13] What tortuous language to concede the MacIver and Furfey point that you can talk to the man and the members of the crowd whereas you can't talk to the paper and the wind! At least we no longer have to contend with tricky principles of parismony.

Another famous controversy was Lundberg's debate with Herbert Blumer over operational definitions.[14] As usual, there is

[12] "The Natural Science Trend in Sociology," *American Journal of Sociology*, 61 (November, 1955), p. 199.

[13] *Ibid.*.

[14] George A. Lundberg, "Operational Definitions in the Social Sciences," *American Journal of Sociology*, 47 (March, 1942), pp. 727-743, and rejoinder by Herbert Blumer, *ibid.*, pp. 743-745. For my own contribution to this controversy, see Harry Alpert, "Operational Definitions in Sociology," *American Sociological*

a certain amount of talking past one another. The issues are multifaceted, but I shall confine this discussion to just two of them: (1) The role of the observer in scientific operations or the "that which" problem; and (2) the quantitative and mensurative issue.

A major element of the Einsteinian revolution in physics was, as I understand it, the introduction of the behavior of the observer as a significant aspect of the analysis of the thing observed. The speed of light, the duration of time, the extension of space all had to be interpreted, in post-Einsteinian physics, in relation to the position of the observer and what he did. Thus, Bridgman, among others, developed a methodological system in which the observable and recordable behavior of the observing scientist becomes an integral part of the analysis of the phenomenon observed.

Lundberg picked up this operational perspective and gave it a special twist, namely, that anything the observer does quantitatively or mensuratively is all right as long as one can record and replicate his behavior. Thus, intelligence can be defined as *that which* intelligence tests measure, or attitude can be defined as *that which* attitude scales record, or social status is *that which* the Chapin scale measures. The "that which" approach has the virtue of fostering precision and clarity, but in Lundberg's hands, it leads to theoretical and conceptual anarchy. Lundberg's formulation of operationalism fails to hold the operating observer responsible for the theoretical and conceptual frameworks within which his operations are developed. His article on operational definitions in the social sciences calls attention, by implication, to a serious omission in the development of operational theory, namely, the failure to create criteria of selection among concepts equally operational and precise. The operations urged by the operationists are of all varieties: mental as well as physical, qualitative as well as quantitative, social and cultural as well as individual, verbal as well as nonverbal. How may one select among them? If we adopt Lundberg's position, namely, that clear and precise terms are to be valued *per se,* we place ourselves in a realm

Review, 3 (December, 1938). pp. 855-861, and "Operational Definitions," *American Journal of Sociology,* 47 (May, 1942), p. 981.

of scientific anarchy. Choice becomes a matter of taste, with every operational anarchist sponsoring his own preferences.

Clarity cannot be the sole standard of scientific conceptualization. Other criteria must be developed. Let us admit, for example, that the more easily one can establish correlationships between a concept and other variables in which one is interested the greater is its value. One may establish an infinity of definitions of "gas," "pressure," and "volume," but the definitions at present in use among physicists are better than others that may be contrived, because it is possible to state, as in Boyle's law, certain relationships among these three variables. Or, let it likewise be admitted that the more empirical data a concept organizes into meaningful relationships, invariant, covariant, dependent, interdependent, etc., the more value it has.

Are not organizing ability and utility, and even meaningfulness, as important in conceptualization as clarity? It is surprising that social scientists of a pragmatic persuasion should espouse concepts and definitions of impeccable clarity but of limited utility and significance. Not just operational definitions, but operational definitions that count, should be our program.[15]

The precision and clarity achieved by defining public opinion as *that which* is reported by a Gallup poll do not absolve the social psychologist from the responsibility of explaining to his fellow scientists why he has selected the particular operations in terms of which he makes his definition.

On the second issue, that of quantification and measurement, Lundberg usually charged his opponents with a *Ding an sich* epistemology and then proceeded to demonstrate that historically things that were not deemed to be subject to quantification and measurement did in fact yield to human ingenuity and were, in fact, quantified and measured. He was particularly skillful in ferreting out unfortunate uses of the word "essential" or "essentially." Say that something was "essentially different" and Lundberg was ready to lower the boom.[16]

[15] Harry Alpert, *American Journal of Sociology,* 47 (May, 1942), p. 981.
[16] Note how he lowers it on Furfey and MacIver and Page, *American Journal*

It is practically impossible in the modern world to believe in Platonic essences. Even Blumer, in rebuttal, denies that he believes that the world is divided into two realms—the quantitative and the qualitative—each with its own inherent and "ultimate" nature. The only issue, as I see it, is one of exclusivity or catholicity: must science be confined and limited to the quantitative and mensurative or may it include the at-the-moment-at-least qualitative and non-measurative? In the name of common-sense, or perhaps personal taste, I opt for the more catholic position. What is gained by tying one's hands in the free quest for truth and understanding? Blumer made the same point as follows: "Our concepts in social psychology are admittedly ambiguous and require increased clarity and preciseness in denotation. This conceptual improvement cannot be secured by a method which would *limit* the meaning of concepts to what is quantitatively and mensuratively determinable, for multitudes of our problems in social psychology are of such a nature as not to be handled by such a method. To force them into a form capable of being treated by such a method may be at the expense of significant empirical items. I believe it desirable to retain concepts, despite their ambiguity, rather than to sacrifice a significant empirical content."[17]

A third polemical area involved the relation of social science to social action. Here Lundberg tangled with Robert S. Lynd in his review of Lynd's "Knowledge for What?"[18] He accepts two of the three main theses presented by Lynd, namely, as Lundberg put it: (1) social science problems tend to be determined not by the criterion of general social usefulness but by the requirements of the existing framework of the scholarly disciplines, as decreed by vested interests of various kinds—the prestige of existing theoretical cults, the absurdities of present departmental organization of the universities and the background and the training

of Sociology, 61 (November, 1955), p. 199 and on Blumer, *American Journal of Sociology,* 47 (March, 1942), pp. 732-733.

[17] Herbert Blumer, *loc. cit.,* p. 745.

[18] *American Journal of Sociology,* 45 (September, 1939), pp. 270-274.

of the scholastic priesthood; and (2) social research should have a more demonstrable relationship to people's basic wants other than the satisfaction of the pure curiosity of the researcher and possibly a small coterie of "scholars" devoted to the pursuit of "knowledge for its own sake."

As would be expected, Lundberg is not prepared to accept without clarification Lynd's third thesis, namely that social scientists should not only analyze and draw inferences but should "implement action." Lundberg is worried about Lynd's criticism of a statement by Wesley C. Mitchell to the effect that "we confine ourselves to stating the facts as we find them. With opinions about the promise or the danger to American life from the growth of trade unions we have no concern as an organization of investigation." Lundberg comments as follows: "Now I would agree that it would be quite within the scientific role for these investigators to indicate the probable effects on the social order of increase or decrease in unionism." At this point Lynd's activist stance becomes too much for Lundberg who asks, "But does Lynd insist that these investigators must also label these effects with the terms promise or danger?"[19] He is obviously unhappy with Lynd's reference to people lecturing on navigation while the ship is going down. Lundberg comments, "From one point of view, it is only because some men were willing to do research and lecture on navigation as their particular ships (individual lives or cultures?) went down (instead of rushing at odd jobs about the ship, which couldn't be saved anyway), that we know a great deal about navigation today. The researches and lectures survived and were found useful on other ships on which, however different they were from ours, men found life quite tolerable and navigation greatly improved."[20] Lundberg can scarcely be identified with the activist wing of American social science, although he concludes the Lynd review by admitting "the essential soundness of the main theme." The latter, he states, "will doubtless cause many owls in collegiate belfries to hoot at this disturbance of their ancient, solitary reign."

[19] *Loc. cit.*, p. 273.
[20] *Loc. cit.*, pp. 273-274.

A fourth polemic that I shall mention briefly was his quarrel with Jessie Bernard over whether science will be used for socially desirable ends.[21] In an exchange with Mrs. Bernard over her article on "The Power of Science and the Science of Power," Lundberg objects to the statement that his advocacy of the wider application of science and of the scientific method in human affairs implies that science will necessarily be used for "socially desirable ends." Lundberg admits that he has *"beliefs and tastes"* about socially desirable ends, but denies the relevance of these beliefs and tastes to questions of scientific validity. He repeats his view that, "There is nothing in scientific work, as such, which dictates to what ends the products of science shall be used" and adds, "nor do I flinch from a single one of 'the more sinister totalitarian implications' (whatever they are) of my conclusions."[22] Then he grudgingly concedes that, "It is true that I have expressed considerable optimism on the probability that science will in fact, on the whole and in the long run, be used for ends that the masses of men desire. . ."[23] Unaware of the inconsistency of his position, he later adds, "The idea that science might be the pan-culturally valid system compelling consensus through the demonstrated validity of its methods is a consummation I contemplate with great satisfaction and some optimism."[24]

Scientism and Polemicism, and their consequences, are, indeed, the key to George A. Lundberg. Unhappily the polemicism frequently impeded the scientism.

Furthermore, the case of George A. Lundberg poses a difficult problem for the sociology of knowledge: does the recourse to scientism correlate positively with political conservatism? I pose this as a question without knowing the answer. However, it strikes me as a reasonable hypothesis that espousal of the *wertfrei* view of science has a relationship to the conservative philosophy. The view that scientific propositions are ethic-free provides one with a ready-made rationalized justification for rejecting social and political causes.

[21] *American Sociological Review,* 14 (December, 1949), pp. 796-801.
[22] *Ibid.,* p. 796.
[23] *Ibid.*
[24] *Ibid.,* p. 797.

Just as patriotism is the last refuge of scoundrels, scientism may be the last refuge of the political conservative. Are all of us in the sociological enterprise because deep in our hearts we are counter-revolutionaries? The student of the science of science, and especially the sociology of science, may well examine the extent to which scientism has functioned as a conservative political ideology. It is very easy for the "scientismist" to eschew involvement in social and political causes on the ground that all the scientific evidence is not yet in. Therefore, isn't our dedication to such causes as world government, United Nations, UNESCO, democracy, freedom, The Great Society, etc., fundamentally "unscientific," and therefore irrational? Lundberg's writings are full of sharp barbs against international organizations and nationalistic movements such as Zionism. I am quite convinced that were he living today he would be hurling his heaviest invective artillery against the Peace Corps, the Job Corps, the anti-poverty program and other features of the Great Society.

By way of example, consider Lundberg's opposition to the action of the American Sociological Society in September, 1950, at its annual meeting in Denver, in submitting a resolution deploring the loyalty oath required by the University of California.[25] Lundberg objected to the resolution on the ground that the American Sociological Society is a scientific society and not a pressure group. He stated in his letter to the editor of the *American Sociological Review* that he has no objection to belonging to pressure groups, but that he does object to pressure groups masquerading as scientific societies. This is a curious dichotomy if it is intended to imply that scientific societies have no responsibility for concerning themselves with the social, economic, political, and intellectual conditions which promote or impede science as a social institution. Must scientific societies stand idly by as they see themselves destroyed or impeded in their scientific endeavors? A scientific society *is*, willy-nilly, a pressure group for science.[26]

[25] *American Sociological Review*, 15 (December, 1950), p. 782. The text of the resolution is given in the same issue at pp. 786-787.

[26] Another letter on the same issue was written by my former colleague at the

There is a necessary ethos of science. Is it "unscientific" to support the conditions that make possible the scientific enterprise? Lundberg seems here to be espousing a totally unsociological, unnatural, and unreal, virginal view of science. In any case, he finds himself on the conservative side of the issue.

(Lundberg, incidentally, is at his vitriolic best in objecting to the passing of resolutions at the business meeting of the Society. He writes: "The practice of passing resolutions in the name of the American Sociological Society at the small rump session attended by a negligible percentage of the total membership, plus whatever number of book salesmen, clerks, and other hotel personnel may happen to be present or who may be brought in for voting purposes, is utterly indefensible and unnecessary.")[27]

Another example is Lundberg's views on democracy and dictatorship. He states that he shall continue to resist "the totalitarian trend" because he dislikes it. However, he asserts that it is a fact that dictators come into power and maintain themselves only with popular support. "I refer specifically to the fact, and I believe it is a fact, that dictators too do not come into being and operate for any length of time entirely without considerable popular support and, perhaps, with the support of the overwhelming majority of the underlying population."[28] Asserting that something *is* a fact and then describing the fact as a *perhaps* is illogical enough. I am concerned at this moment, however, with the proposition that really, deep-down, dictators are gentlemen with popular support.

Lundberg admits that he has a democratic bias, but insists that it is only a bias and not a scientific conclusion. Yet he doubts whether the "rising generation" will share his bias. He thinks that "they (the rising generation) will regard many of my concerns for minorities as sentimental nonsense, incompatible with the kind of integrated behavior required in a technologically more ad-

---

Bureau of the Budget, Dr. W. Edwards Deming. *Ibid.*, p. 783. Deming, too, urges that "as a Society, we should stick to science."

[27] *Ibid.*, p. 782.

[28] *American Sociological Review*, 14 (December, 1949), p. 797.

vanced society. My nostalgic views to the contrary are probably obsolete."[29] Good grief, George! Aren't you saying that democracy is incompatible with the requirements of technologically advanced society?

It is indeed quite ironic that, as sociology has become more scientific, partly as a result of Lundberg's influence and partly as a result of the noble convergences in sociological theory identified by Lundberg in the works of Lazarsfeld and Merton, Parsons and Bales and Stouffer, and Dodd and Lundberg,[30] it seems to have become more irrelevant to the social issues of the day. I recently visited with the sociology department of a well-known university. The department was concerned with identifying an interest or perspective in terms of which it might mobilize its resources in a thrust toward becoming a top ranking department. I suggested that it become the best possible department in what I called compassionate sociology. The notion was strongly resisted, if not rejected outright, on the ground that any department of sociology that did not have a strong scientific image was condemned to second class status. Saint George, thou hast, indeed, worked well thy wonders to perform!

Yet, Lundberg himself was a compassionate man. I realize that one cannot erect a social philosophy out of a personality trait, but I believe that it is relevant to note that, however irascible Lundberg may have appeared to be at sociological conventions, and however dogmatic he may have appeared to be in his never ending polemical battles, he was, at heart, a humanistic man of compassion. Listen to the testimony of Lucy Freeman in her autobiographical "Fight Against Fears":[31]

"Some of our more kindly professors tried to help the unhappy students. One gentle man reassured us, 'The capacity of the human

[29] *Ibid.*

[30] See George A. Lundberg, "Some Convergences in Sociological Theory," *American Journal of Sociology,* 62 (July, 1956), pp. 21-27, and George A. Lundberg, "The Natural Science Trend in Sociology," *American Journal of Sociology,* 61 (November, 1955), esp. p. 202, footnote 27.

[31] Lucy Freeman, *Fight Against Fears,* New York: Pocket Books, 1967, pp. 181-183. Miss Freeman does not mention Lundberg by name.

race to endure suffering is vastly underestimated.' He should know, for he had a cough that, at times, theatened to tear him apart." Later, Miss Freeman describes her ordeal during a comprehensive oral examination. "The quiet gentle bachelor sat reading a newspaper all through my inquisition as though to say, 'Don't worry, this is just another minor tribulation which we must endure.' " His stoic nature clearly shows through in these reports, but Lundberg is true to form in Miss Freeman's recording of the reply of a "favorite social studies professor" to a parent's charge of "scientism."

"Madam," the professor replied, "we can make no attempt to measure the cellular structure of the Holy Ghost."[32] That, I am sure, put Madam in her place (and perhaps prompted her to remove her daughter from Bennington's evil influences).

I started with a one word summary of Lundberg's social philosophy. I actually needed four: scientism, polemicism, conservatism, humanism.

George Lundberg, we salute you. Your influence on sociology was truly seminal. You made our discipline intellectually exciting. You were, in the etymological sense of the word, inspirational. You breathed life into sociology. I can see you now trying to explain to God that He doesn't really exist because no one has measured Him, or, perhaps, explaining to Him that, if He does exist, He is *that which* is checked as a verbal symbol on an equal-appearing interval attitude scale. You are undoubtedly reading papers to the Celestial Sociological Association on the importance of an operational mathematical approach to the question of how many angels can sit on the head of a pin. And you must be writing letters to the editor of the Celestial Sociological Review thanking him for his general agreement with your views on natural science, but regretfully pointing out some minor errors. That companion volume, you insist was written by Dodd, not God.

[32] Cf. *Foundations of Sociology*, p. 31: "It is not necessary for a priest to give an account of the cellular structure of the Holy Ghost."

PART II

Neo-Behaviorism and the Behavioral Sciences

PAUL KURTZ

Are the behavioral sciences a mere intellectual fashion of the first half of the twentieth century, or on the contrary do they have something significant to say for the traditional study of man?

Even a cursory examination of the behavioral sciences as they exist today demonstrates the great energy that is being expended in these fields. The behavioristic study of man is a vast enterprise and the sheer number of behavioral scientists, journals, institutes and organizations devoted to the task is enormous. George Lundberg had contributed significantly to the development of the behavioral sciences in the United States.

Yet the whole behavioral science approach stands out in sharp contrast to the methods still being used to study human beings in various parts of the world, i.e., the traditional humanistic study of man. Indeed, the behaviorist approach is widely criticized by philosophers, theologians, classicists and humanists as fundamentally misdirected in nature and scope. One hears a great deal about the narrowness of the statistical, or experimental method *vis a vis* the need for theory, or the insufficient appreciation of an historical focus, or more recently the need for a phenomenological approach to probe the *lebenswelt* and of the importance of linguistic analysis.

In no small measure a good deal of the criticism is based upon a misunderstanding of the nature of "behaviorism," "neo-behaviorism" and the "behavioral sciences." Far from being a passing style, a dramatic revolution has occurred in the twentieth century study of man, with which it would be well for critics of the behavioral sciences to acquaint themselves.

I. BEHAVIORISM AND NEO-BEHAVIORISM

The term "behaviorism" was first used in the early part of the twentieth century within psychology. As a result, "behavioral science" is often mistakenly identified with psychology. This is unfortunate, since the behavioral program of the twentieth century has been extended to many other sciences. Moreover, "behaviorism" was first interpreted in its physicalist and hence most extreme sense; but there is now a non-reductive aspect to the behaviorist program that has a wider appeal. For these reasons it is appropriate to designate the new behaviorism which one finds in the behaviorial sciences today as "neo-behaviorism."

Historically two main forms of behaviorism have developed: mechanistic and functional. Watson and Pavlov are chiefly responsible for first enunciating mechanistic behaviorism. All human or animal behavior, it was alleged, was to be accounted for in terms of physical explanations; and all psychological processes were to be correlated with observable physical changes in the organism on the micro and molar level. Introspection as a psychological method was held inadmissible. There was no need to postulate a mysterious "mind" or "subject." Thus psychology was interpreted as a natural or biological science in which only mechanistic causal explanations were admitted.

Functional behaviorism on the other hand was a weaker version of the same movement. It was originally defended by American pragmatists such as James, Dewey, and Mead and psychologists such as E. S. Tolman and C. L. Hull. These functionalists likewise rejected a mind-body dualism and were critical of any attempt to deal with consciousness as a substantive entity. They cast suspicion on introspective psychological reports which were untested or uncorrelated with observable behavior. But unlike the mechanistic behaviorists they did not believe that simple physicalist explanations would suffice. Rather, they said that human behavior was goal-directed or purposive, and hence that teleonomic[1] and functional explanations were useful in dealing with human behavior, and that since man was a social animal it was necessary that biological behaviorism be supplemented by social behaviorism. These latter day behaviorists are sometimes called transactionalists, because they have held that human beings transact within a biological and social environment, and that any adequate account of behavior must deal with the full field of interaction. Accordingly, behaviorists became interested in social psychology, sociology and cultural anthropology as aspects of the transactional field.

The term "behaviorism" originally introduced within psychology has since been extended to the other sciences which deal with man, so that today the term "behavioral science" has wider application. Indeed, the new behavioral program may now be said to apply to virtually all the sciences and specialities which deal with man; and at least thirteen such fields of investigation can be discriminated. A recent study has shown that all of the older fields now have their behaviorists.[2] Moreover, a veritable breakthrough has occurred in the past two decades by the establishment of a whole set of "newer" fields, which are unashamedly behavioral and which deal with areas traditionally philosophical, such as language, meaning and value.

Earlier behaviorism had been thought by many to provide a theory of human nature, i.e., a set of general assumptions about the nature of man. And this was probably true to some extent; for behaviorism generally had been allied to a materialistic or naturalistic conception of the universe and behaviorists have been opposed to the postulation of any "subjective consciousness," "mind," "self," or "soul" separate and distinct from the body.

[1] A form of teleological explanation, yet devoid of traditional metaphysical overtones.

[2] *A Current Appraisal of the Behavioral Sciences,* by Rollo Handy and Paul Kurtz, Behavioral Research Council, Great Barrington, Massachusetts, 1964.

Behaviorism had focussed on behavior and on the field of interaction, implying that transactive behavior, action, processes or events are the basic constitutive "reality" of human beings.

Most present-day neo-behaviorists, however, would regard any such theoretical account as premature and metaphysical speculation. Neo-behaviorism, they would insist, should be interpreted primarily as introducing a set of regulative principles which recommend *how* we should go about studying human beings. The neo-behaviorists are interested in proposing prescriptive rules for investigating man, not in offering general accounts of his "essential traits," "nature" or "being." Thus neo-behaviorism is best construed as a strategy of research or a methodological program.

What does the neo-behavioral program involve? Unfortunately no precise platform has been worked out which would be acceptable to all of its proponents. What is clear is that neo-behaviorism cannot be identified simply with the Pavlovian-Watsonian program of physicalist reductionism; nor is neo-behaviorism today to be identified with any one school in psychology, such as the SR conditioned response learning theory. The restricted definition of "behaviorism" which a B. F. Skinner in psychology might employ would hardly be acceptable to a neo-behaviorist in political science, sociology or economics. Virtually all neo-behaviorists, including even the most extreme physicalist behaviorists of earlier days, are now willing to deal with psychological areas which were formerly considered *verboten,* such as perception, thinking and motivation, and they recognize the importance of introspective reports as psychological data to be explained. Some of the recent advocates of neo-behaviorism are also receptive to the use of teleonomic, functional, intentional and motive explanations. Many do not believe that a reduction of the many sciences of man to a single physical science is at this stage of research possible or even desirable.

Some critics have interpreted behaviorism as "logical behaviorism," that is, as a theory of meaning in which every statement or definition of a psychological fact is equivalent to or must be translated into some statement of a physical fact. Others have interpreted behaviorism as an operationalist theory of definition whereby all definitions admitted into behavioral science must be framed in terms of a set of operations to be performed. But these interpretations of neo-behaviorism are also far too restrictive and would exclude a great number of inquirers who would wish to be considered as participating in the neo-behavioral program. It is clear that for the neo-behaviorist only a looser theory of meaning and definition is possible. He does not insist that all sentences in behavioral science be directly stated in physicalist or operational terms, but simply that they be related to other sentences which are, thus allowing for the admission of intervening variables and hypothetical constructs. Logical behaviorism and operationalism are wedded to early versions of logical positivism and pragmatism, both of which have been superseded.

We have said what the neo-behaviorist program is not, may we say more directly what it is?: What is crucial to neo-behaviorism is simply the insistence that all hypotheses introduced in science must be *experimentally confirmable and that these verifications must be intersubjectively or publicly repeatable by the community of inquirers.*

While neo-behaviorists stress the role of experimental verification as essential to all scientific inquiry, this in no way precludes the use of mathematical models and theoretical systems, which all but the most extreme empiricists concede to be essential to any developed science. Many behavioral scientists today are reluctant to build high level theoretical deductive systems, which they frequently consider to smack of premature philosophical speculation or intuitive guesswork. They prefer to concentrate upon the data and upon detailed experimental observation and statistical correlation. Most take as their immediate goal the development of hypotheses of the middle range, i.e., hypotheses amenable to some theoretical generality, yet closely related to concrete empirical contexts or particular facts. Yet behavioral science like natural and biological science has as its eventual goal the development of a set of mutually related hypotheses of wider deductive and theoretical significance. In the last analysis, however, neo-behaviorists insist that all statements that are considered warranted must be experimentally confirmed by reference to publicly observable changes.

II. THE BEHAVIORAL SCIENCES

The most remarkable fact about the neo-behavioristic program today is that it is shared by so many different inquirers in a variety of disciplines, each of which is considered to be a behavioral science. The traditional fields of science, which have now become in part behavioristic are familiar: anthropology, sociology, psychology, political science, economics, jurisprudence, education and history. The newer fields which have recently developed are less well-known: the communication sciences, including linguistics, cybernetics, and information theory and the preferential sciences, such as decision making and game theory.

We are faced with the complex question of the definition of the field of each science and of its interrelations with the other sciences. The sciences of man are today dependent upon the division of labor that has evolved, largely in the University context; but this is an historical development which is in part accidental and not based upon viable reasons. The neo-behaviorist insists that the present division of inquiry is in need of fundamental reorganization. Indeed the definitions of the separate sciences border at times on chaos. Moreover, the duplication of effort between the sciences suggests an inefficient expenditure of talent.

For example, both anthropology and sociology claim to be "integrating" sciences, but the precise differences between them are at times difficult to ascertain. The anthropologist, Ralph Linton, for example, defined his field in general terms as "the science of man," and A. L. Kroeber thought that it aims at being "a coordinating science." Yet the sociologist Stuart Dodd also claims that sociology is a general science which deals "with the general characteristics of human groups in space and time."[3] A similar problem may be raised for the definition of history. Many have defined history

[3] *Systematic Social Science: A Dimensional Sociology,* Beirut, Lebanon, 1947, p. 2.

very loosely—thus Henri Pirenne says that the "object of the study of history is the development of human societies in space and time."[4] Henri Berr and Lucien Febvre have said, however, that "no branch of knowledge. . . has exhibited more varied modalities and answered to more contradictory conceptions than has history."[5] The definition of economics is also in trouble. For Alfred Marshall, economics is "a study of man's actions in the ordinary business of life."[6] Ludwig von Mises, however, considers it to be "a branch of the more general theory of human action."[7] While for Jacob Viner, economics "is whatever economists do." Among the newer fields of behavioral research the duplication of effort is very noticeable. Game theory is often considered part of decision making, which is interpreted as part of operations research, management science or administration theory. And communication and information theory are frequently identified with cybernetics or systems engineering. In addition, the lines between the older and the newer sciences are not always clearly drawn. For example, both economics and political science today have incorporated game theory and decision theory as part of their inquiries.

Can any sense be made of the present proliferation of the behavioral sciences? Specialization up to a point may be convenient, but no science can be developed entirely independently of the other sciences without becoming itself an obstacle to further inquiry.

With this problem in mind it will be convenient to provide a list of the basic behavioral sciences. This list is not exhaustive.[8] It does touch on the main disciplines which can be observed in a rapidly growing area of research. The list is intended to provide,

[4] Quoted in Berr and Febvre, "History" in *Encyclopaedia of the Social Sciences.*

[5] *Ibid.*

[6] *Principles of Economics,* New York, Macmillan, Vol. 7, 1890, p. 1.

[7] *Human Action, A Treatise on Economics,* New Haven, Yale University, 1949.

[8] There are other fields that may qualify as behavioral. For example, *Geography* studies environments as they relate to man. Moreover, some of the subfields of the traditional behavioral sciences may become separate fields. Some may also consider *General Systems Theory* to be a behavioral science, though others would exclude it since it is more theoretical than experimental.

from the standpoint of the neo-behaviorists, tentative working definitions of the subject matters of the separate sciences, as well as some indication of the interrelations of these sciences with cognate sciences. The interrelationship of these behavioral sciences is a special problem, however, to which we shall return in Section III.

THE TRADITIONAL FIELDS

Anthropology. Traditionally "the comparative study of man and his works," neo-behavioristic anthropologists today investigate the biological, and especially the cultural aspects of humans from the earliest origins until the present day. Anthropology may be divided into two subfields: (a) *physical anthropology:* a study of the evolution and present biological properties of human species and the interrelation between biological variability and cultural setting, and (b) *cultural anthropology* (*ethnology* or *social anthropology*): the study of the development and function of customs and techniques of the organization and functioning of cultures, their stability and change, similarities and differences. Anthropology is also closely related to two others: (c) *archaeology*: the study of past human cultures and the analysis of the relations between culture, environment, technology and population size, and (d) *linguistics*: the inquiry into human languages as they relate to culture.[9] The relation of anthropology to sociology, biology, psychology and history is especially close.

Sociology. Sociologists study the behavior of humans in social groups and organizations and the way these groups are structured and function. This involves a study of customs, habits, mores, social disorganization, social change and problems of social roles and statuses. Among the closely related subfields are: (a) *social psychology*: the psychology and personality aspects of social interaction, and (b) *population and human ecology or demography*: a study of population trends and migration patterns. Sociology

[9] Linguistics is treated separately below.

is closely related to anthropology, political science, history, psychology and economics.

Psychology. As inquiry into both human and animal behavior, psychologists focus on the individual, though relating individual characteristics to the social and environmental context. Psychology emphasizes the complex biological functions of humans, such as perception, learning, thinking, attitudes, aptitudes, emotion, motivation. Among the important subfields of psychology are: (a) *social psychology*: a study of social groups and their effect on variables of individual behavior, (b) *developmental psychology*: the study of processes of development, especially in the child, (c) *comparative psychology*: the study of similarities and differences between animals and human beings, and (d) *psychoanalysis*: a study of unconscious processes as they influence behavior. There is considerable controversy as to whether psychoanalysis is or can be reformulated as a behavioral science. Only a limited portion of psychoanalytic inquiry presently can be construed as behavioristic. Psychology is related to biology and physiology, sociology and anthropology.

Political Science. Traditionally the investigation of political institutions and power with emphasis on the structure and functioning of governments, more recently political scientists study the processes of decision and power within a social or intellectual community. A closely related subfield is *public administration*: the structure and function of institutions and their administration, especially those publicly organized. Political science is related to economics, history, jurisprudence, psychology and sociology.

Economics. Originally defined as "the science of wealth," more recently in terms of "scarcity," economists investigate how men and society choose to employ scarce productive resources to produce commodities with or without the use of money and exchange, and to distribute them for consumption. Among the areas for special study are price, business cycles, money and banking, finance, economic growth and development, labor, farm and consumer groups and international trade. Economics is closely related to politics, jurisprudence, sociology, history, psychology, game and decision theory.

Jurisprudence. Traditionally a part of the philosophy of law, jurisprudence today is an inquiry into legal processes, rules and organizations, particularly of judicial, legislative and executive behavior. Jurisprudence is closely related to political science, history, economics, sociology and anthropology.

Education. Education is especially concerned with the teaching and learning process and of social means of facilitating this, particularly in terms of the school. Education is intimately related to psychology and sociology.

History. Historians concentrate upon the dated sequences of particular events in the past, their correlation, description and explanation. A special problem that arises is the difference between history and the other sciences. Many think history an art, or a form of literature, or so irreducibly concerned with the unique that it cannot provide descriptive or explanatory causal laws. But historians who are neo-behaviorists insist that there is a mutual relationship between history and the behavioral sciences. Historians utilize the tested hypotheses of the behavioral sciences to deal with concrete problems of the past. History is thus closely related to archaeology, anthropology, political science, economics, sociology, jurisprudence and psychology.

THE NEWER FIELDS

Some of the questions that the newer fields of behavioral science deal with have been investigated for centuries, yet it is only comparatively recently that efforts have been made to apply behavioral techniques. The problems of knowledge and language have traditionally been considered philosophical questions. In the past two decades a great deal of attention has been devoted by behavioral inquirers to the formulation of testable hypotheses.

The Communication Sciences

Linguistics. Linguistics historically was considered a subject for classicists, philologists and grammarians. Today there is a small group of intensive inquirers concerned with developing descriptive linguistics. This entails an inquiry into language structures, the relationships between languages and their historical changes. Linguists study the principles underlying the organization of languages, the system of sounds and the ways in which words and sentences are formed. Linguistics has a special affinity to anthropology.

Cybernetics. Cybernetics is an inquiry into the regulative processes of physical, biological and behavioral systems, with special emphasis on feedback mechanics in nervous systems and machines. According to Norbert Weiner, the founder of cybernetics, it is concerned with "the entire field of control and communication theory, whether in the machine or in the animal."[10] Cybernetic engineers have been successful in applying electronic techniques to the creation of automatic systems. In regard to humans, the chief explanatory hypothesis that is used is the notion that the brain and central nervous system operate like these machines. Thus, complex machines can be constructed which parallel human functions: they can play chess, detect and correct their errors, store and sort information, etc. The basic explanatory hypothesis introduced is that of negative feedback, i.e., the work done by a feedback mechanism opposes the direction of the brain system and thus serves to regulate it. The brain thus operates something like a thermostat or governor on a machine. Cybernetics is closely connected to biology and physiology and to the field of electronics in the natural sciences.

Information Theory. This is sometimes used synonymously with "communication theory." Information theorists inquire into the most effective ways of coding, transmitting and receiving messages in communication systems. They are especially interested in the

[10] *Cybernetics,* New York, Wiley, 1948, p. 19.

technology of speed, accuracy and economic cost of transmission. They believe that quantitative and statistical measurements can be applied to communication channels and signals and that this information will be of use in explaining human knowledge. This field is a highly developed part of natural science technology.

The Preferential Sciences

Game Theory. An inquiry into human situations which are analogous to games and in which choices are made among alternative strategies by "rational" individuals in conflict or competition. There is special effort to formulate mathematical models which are supposed to explain and predict human conduct in such specialized situations. This inquiry is now being used within economics and political science.

Decision Making Theory. An investigation of those aspects of human behavior in which choices are made among alternatives. Efforts are made to (a) describe and explain the decision making process, and also (b) to develop criteria for measuring the relative importance of goals by considerations of probability, effectiveness and value. This field is sometimes identified as Value Theory, Operations Research, Systems Engineering, and Management Science. Decision making inquiry is related to all the sciences, but especially to psychology, economics and political science.

III. THE OVERLAPPING OF THE BEHAVIORAL SCIENCES

There is so much overlapping among the behavioral sciences that one may ask: Is there one science of man, of which these various fields are only parts, or are these fields necessarily separate and distinct?

The same problem had been raised during the development of the social sciences, and there are, of course, several suggestions. A nineteenth century basis for the distinction between the social sciences was in terms of institutions. Thus it was alleged that political science is distinguished from the other sciences by the fact that it studies "the state" and "the government," whereas economics deals with "the economy," education with "the school," and sociology with "the family," "the church" and other social institutions as they interact in society as a whole. This division, while suggestive, is nonetheless fraught with difficulty for the neo-behaviorist, who is especially disturbed about the vague term "institution," a notion which he considers to be in some of its formulations an Hegelian abstraction incapable of precise behavioral definition. Moreover, he asks, where would this analysis leave psychology, the communication and preferential sciences, many of which do not in all of their inquiries deal with the institutional setting?

Another suggestion is that all the sciences, including the natural and biological sciences, be divided up in terms of "levels" of organization. The general system theorists are especially sympathetic with this view: the natural sciences they claim, deal with microparticles on the level of sub-atomic and atomic events, and the biological sciences with the cell and the organ. Psychology studies the individual as he functions in an environment. Each of the separate sciences treats various forms of higher level organizations and groups: political science with governmental organizations; economics with specialized organizations that produce, market, and consume; sociology and anthropology with the interaction of these groups in society or in the culture as a whole. The communication and preferential sciences could find appropriate levels in the scheme. Information theory could view messages in terms of "information quanta," linguistics would deal with language as a cultural phenomenon, and decision making might be construed both in biological and sociological terms. Most behavioral scientists are dubious of basing the division of inquiry upon this ground, for it would seem to commit the behavioral sciences to an imprecise and unverified *a priori* metaphysical theory of emergent levels. Neo-behaviorism on the contrary would prefer to be neutral as far as possible in its ontological presuppositions, which it believes are not relevant to the practice of inquiry.

Some have suggested that the behavioral sciences might be distinguished empirically by the fact that they focus on different aspects of behavior: political science on the processes of decision making and the exercise of power by governmental officials; economics on producing, marketing and consuming behavior; sociology on familial, religious and educational processes and functions; psychology on certain highly specialized processes of the individual, such as motivation, perceiving, thinking, etc. But this division, while more attractive than the institutional or level theories, may pose similar difficulties. Individual and social behavior can *not* be easily dissected or abstracted, since the subject matter is continuous; any such division presupposes a general theory before inquiry, which may prejudice inquiry.

For the neo-behaviorists, the overriding consideration of how to divide inquiry is that of *convenience:* which strategy of research is most likely to be most fruitful in achieving the aim of explanation and prediction. All recognize that while some degree of specialization of the sciences is surely useful and necessary, in actuality any hard and fast line that may develop may do much to impede behavioral research and the lines between the sciences must be constantly redrawn. Most behaviorists would insist that the present division of inquiry is neither sacrosanct nor infallible. The great danger is that the definitions of the sciences in one age may become ossified by tradition and oppose new departures in inquiry in the future.

The basic consideration should always be: what is the best strategy for organizing cooperative research? Today the most promising organization of research energy seems to be not simply in terms of separate disciplines, but in terms of *common problems.* Thus the neo-behaviorist recognizes that the immediate imperative for him is to bring to bear the combined talents and resources of many separate sciences to the treatment of those problems which are interdisciplinary in character.

IV. INTERDISCIPLINARY PROBLEMS

As one examines the recent literature, one finds indeed that there are a number of interdisciplinary problems which have emerged and which are common to many behavioral sciences. I can only list some of the most significant.

Study of language and communication. The established sciences such as psychology, social and political science and anthropology have turned their attention to the investigation of symbolic and verbal behavior. In these inquiries they have been aided by the newer sciences of communications, especially by linguistics, cybernetics and information theory. Many areas of thinking and cognition have been explored as aspects of verbal behavior. B. F. Skinner's book, *Verbal Behavior,*[11] is typical of one such approach to traditional questions of meaning and significance. The point is that the study of language and communication is not the private province of any one science, but of many. A great number of techniques have been used, including statistics, comparative analyses, crosscultural inquiries and field studies.

Personality, acculturation, socialization, learning. Similarly, social, clinical and experimental psychology, anthropology, psychoanalysis, biology, sociology and education have all focused on the problem of personality development: what are the factors and characteristics involved in personality learning and development. There have been extensive inquiries of child development and animal behavior employing mathematical statistics, projective tests, comparative analyses, cross-cultural and field studies.

Social structure, function and mobility. Sociologists have introduced the concepts of structure, function, role and status in an effort to explain social systems. These concepts have also been used by anthropologists, social psychologists and political scientists. Various techniques have been used such as statistical, scaling devices and comparative studies to study specific situations: the government, the school, the community, the church, the economy, the military, etc.

Small group interaction. This area of social interaction provides a rich field for cooperative research. Social psychologists, sociologists, educational inquirers and organization theorists have

[11] New York, Appleton-Century-Crofts, 1957.

turned to such topics because of the greater facility for controlled laboratory situations and test of hypotheses.

The policy sciences, decision, preference, value. The newer behavioral sciences are concerned with describing how human beings make decisions and choices and in also offering guidance in policy formation, rule and prescription making. Linear programming, systems engineering, decision, organization and game theorists have suggested that there are mathematical-logical models for predicting choices and guiding policy. They have introduced high level probability and statistical models, and have employed computer techniques. The older social sciences have attempted to use these methods, particularly economics, political science and sociology; and they, along with education and jurisprudence, have been called, not inappropriately, by H. D. Lasswell, "the policy sciences."

Administrative and organization theory. This is a rapidly growing area, largely under the influence of Herbert A. Simon, which deals with organizations, their administrative structures and the way they function. Political scientists, sociologists and economists have participated in this inquiry.

Attitudes, opinion, consumer wants. A major advance has been achieved by the use of public opinion polls, sampling, interviewing techniques, scaling devices, models, etc. in describing and accounting for public attitudes and opinion. Political scientists, sociologists, economists, and psychologists have especially contributed to this inquiry.

Biological basis of behavior. A veritable breakthrough has been achieved in molecular biology and in uncovering the physical-chemical basis of behavior. Thus research into DNA or RNA, the electrical stimulation of the brain, and the use of drugs to modify behavior, has had great impact in psychology, psychiatry and medicine and indeed in the study of group behavior in sociology.

The above is only a partial list of the convergence or interest among many behavioral sciences on many broad frontier problems. But, of course, behavioral science continues to focus on problems more particular in character, such as economic growth and development, population control, demography and human ecology, juvenile delinquency, urban planning, international relations and conflict resolution. The prospect in the behavioral sciences is that there will be greater team work and cooperative inquiry in the future. In this sense twentieth century behavioral science is following a pattern which has already become a strong force in natural science where teams of researchers from many fields contribute to the solution of particular problems.

There have been a great number of gains in the behavioral sciences in recent decades by means of cooperative inquiry, much of which is unknown to those outside of the field. Among some of the most interesting have been: the use of Carbon 14 dating in anthropology, archaeology and history to verify the age of artifacts and fossil remains, electrical and chemical stimulation of the brain as a means of modifying psychological and group behavior, the creating of cybernetic machine models as clues to the functioning of the human brain, the use of statistical techniques in linguistics and anthropology for analyzing languages and rates of change ("lexico-statistical dating"), the building of econometric and game models as indices to economic behavior, the effective statistical characterization and prediction of public opinion attitudes, and the development of teaching machines and programmed instruments in education.

V. IS A UNITY OF THE SCIENCES POSSIBLE?

A fundamental issue often raised in the behavioral sciences is whether the remarkable convergence of interest and focus of the many different fields suggests that a single behavioral science of man is an achievable ideal. The unity of the sciences ideal has aroused the imaginative dedication of many of the best scientific minds, at least as far back as the 16th and 17th centuries. This has meant for many not only a unity of the behavioral sciences but of all the sciences, with the reduction of the behavioral sciences to the biological sciences and of these sciences to the natural sciences.

This program, often called *reductionism,* has as its eventual goal a unity of language, but also, and more fundamentally, a unity of the hypotheses and laws of the sciences. Thus, for example, laws derived in biology, psychology or sociology are alleged to be only sub-instances of more general laws.

Most of those who have defended reductionism have been physicalists in that they have conceived of the basic laws and propositions of science as ultimately definable in physical terms. There have been, however, other nonphysicalist advocates of reductionism. Methodological individualists have argued that the laws of the social sciences were translatable into psychological and biological laws governing the individual. Those defending a sociological interpretation of history seem to make sociology or economics the dominant science. And organicists opt for biology.

Important advances have been made in the direction of reductionism, particularly of physicalist reductionism. For example, physics and chemistry have been closely interrelated, as have psychology and biology in many important areas. But no one would affirm that the reductionist ideal has been fully achieved as yet. Reductionism is not primarily a tested theory of the universe, so much as it is a *methodological ideal or program.* That is, like neobehaviorism, reductionism may be construed as providing a set of prescriptive rules and recommendations that a certain line of inquiry be undertaken in the future.

There have been strong criticisms leveled against this program from a variety of fields. Organismic biologists have resisted the reduction of biology *in toto* to chemistry or physics, claiming that the principle of organization of an organic system is not explainable entirely by reference to its simpler parts. Holists have maintained that the body functions as a whole not reducible to its components. Gestalt psychologists have insisted that the holistic interpretation of perception is essential to our understanding of it. Sociologists and anthropologists have objected to the reduction of socio-cultural concepts and hypotheses to methodological individualism or to the psycho-biology of the body; for social relations or the functioning of social systems and organizations are not to be understood simply in terms of the properties of separate individuals.

What is at stake in this controversy is the relationship between the conceptual language *and* laws of the various sciences. Which is correct: the reductive model, which insists that both the language and the laws of the sciences can be reduced to one basic science, or the holistic model, which denies that this can be fully achieved?

The answer from the standpoint of the neo-behaviorist, I think, is that *both* are correct in part and in relation to different aspects of science. If one examines the present state of the behavioral sciences, perhaps only a third model, which I have labeled *coductionism*, accurately describes the present state of inquiry and seems the wisest strategy of research to pursue in the immediate future.[12]

Thus, for many questions that arise in behavioral research, rather than insisting upon the reduction of all explanations to one, *or* upon the autonomy of separate explanations, a variety of explanations from many different sciences may be relevant, and some of these may be reducible, but not all. There are in the behavioral sciences a convergence of mutually supportive concepts and hypotheses from the separate sciences, each of which may provide some aid in explaining one aspect of a situation, yet none of which may have priority. For example, the problem of economic growth and development is one that concerns a number of behavioral sciences. What are the factors which contribute to the growth and development of an area or nation? Economists analyze aspects such as the amount of capital available for investment, natural resources, technology and market potentialities. But this in itself is hardly sufficient. One must call upon the political scientist, who points to the political structure, the attitude of the government toward economic development, whether it encourages expansion or not, or the policies of the various political parties contending for

[12] For an extended treatment of coduction see my book, *Decision and the Condition of Man*, Seattle, Wash., University of Washington Press, 1965, Ch. 5; also "Coduction: A Logic of Explanation in the Behavioral and Social Sciences," in *Proceedings of the XIIIth International Congress of Philosophy*, Mexico City, 1964.

power. But a sociological analysis of public opinion and attitudes or of the class structure is an essential ingredient necessary to understand the growth rate. Similarly, the level of development of educational facilities, or the influence of psychological and value attitudes towards economic growth rates are relevant. Hence the total situation is a function of a variety of causal conditions and each of the behavioral sciences introduces relevant factors. There may not be a single causal explanation which is ultimate and decisive in regard to economic change. The logic of *coduction* suggests that what is needed are mutually supportive explanations from many contexts of analysis rather than a single deductive model.

Interdisciplinary work thus is essential to behavioral research. Yet I do not wish to suggest that this reference to autonomous explanations of the sciences precludes the reductive ideal. Coduction is a regulative principle of inquiry allowing a variety of explanations—but this does not mean that it is more sympathetic to holism—for it allows for the ideal of both reductionism and holism at the same time.

There are no simple rules which tell us which explanations are applicable in any single inquiry; and the criteria of relevance are situational and contextual. One can not say beforehand what to include or exclude. This is a function of the concrete problem at hand. That is why the attempt of either reductive or holistic programs to exclude the other from consideration is legislative censorship, which, I suspect, is based in some measure upon metaphysical poetry of what behavioral science must be like in terms of a preconceived notion of the universe. Only an experimental test of an explanation can determine for the behaviorist what is relevant in regard to any particular frame of reference.

As is clear from our discussion throughout this paper, interdisciplinary inquiry is the lifeblood of behavioral research today, but such research falls short of the call for a unity of the sciences or the disciplines which study man or of the reduction of these sciences to one science.

Yet if it is to be carried on effectively two prerequisites would seem to be necessary. First, even if one cannot as yet have a unity of the concepts and language of all the sciences there is some need for the standardization of terminology and concepts across the behavioral sciences. If behavioral scientists are to be able to communicate effectively with each other, then one of the obstacles to this, namely the development of isolated literatures and different conceptual foundations, must be overcome. It is usually very difficult for one outside of a field to penetrate its jargon, yet similar problems are often faced within other behavioral sciences which have different sets of terms and concepts. Accordingly, as far as possible, efforts should be made to translate cognate terms and concepts into standard usages.

Second, there is a need to concentrate upon the development of hypotheses of the middle range, as Robert K. Merton and Thomas H. Marshall have suggested. Rather than place all reliance upon a quest for high level integrating theories, it may be useful at this stage of behavioral science to concentrate upon hypotheses which have some theoretical generality and yet have some relationship to observable and testable data.

One final problem often raised, which I wish to treat briefly, concerns the relationship of the neo-behaviorist program itself to other seemingly different approaches to the study of man. I am thinking here of the phenomenological and the linguistic-analytic programs which have been introduced within philosophy in the twentieth century and now have advocates in many of the sciences which study man. Following Husserl, the phenomenologists reject the behavioral method as inadequate for treating the *lebenswelt* and accuse it of psychologism (or sociologism), insisting that only a phenomenological account of the given can suffice. Following Wittgenstein, many (but not all) philosophical analysts believe that the key to mentality is language and that language analysis is not reducible to behavioristic methodology. Instead they make a fundamental distinction between "behavior," which they say can be scientifically treated and "action," which involves motivation concepts, and they say cannot be so treated.

It is important to see that due in part to this challenge the neo-behavioral program has been modified: it need not exclude phenomenological reports, linguistic analyses or motivational concepts. Indeed, present day neo-behaviorists have come such a long way from the early strictures of behaviorism that many now *insist* that an important and indeed essential part of the data of behavioral inquiry is the phenomenological given, which cannot be ignored, and linguistic behavior, which is at the center of human behavior. To exclude either on *a priori* grounds is to impoverish and distort at its inception the sciences of man. The principle of coduction, I submit, would allow the behavioral sciences to draw important findings from both phenomenological and linguistic inquiries.

The chief point of difference with phenomenology and linguistic analysis, and it is a serious one, concerns *how to deal with* the phenomenological given and language and how to test assertions about them. The behaviorist insists that all statements about this range of data must be testable by publicly observable inquiry and that a subjective or inituitive approach to either is hardly scientific. He believes, however, that it *is* possible to develop techniques for correlating such subject matter with observable phenomena and of testing assertions about it as a form of behavior.

In Europe and other parts of the world the behavioral sciences have not reached the level of specialization and development that they have in the United States. Sociology is often related to history and psychology to philosophy and these are humanistic rather than scientific in approach. Moreover, the lines between the various disciplines that study man have not been clearly drawn and the specializations are in an underdeveloped state. The behaviorist considers all of this to be seriously deficient.

The rapid specialization and development of the behavioral sciences in recent years, however, have presented serious problems to the behavioral sciences, which the humanities at least do not face: How draw together what has been dissevered? How unify the language and the hypotheses of the separate disciplines? The challenge of the behavioral sciences is to become more interdisciplinary by focusing on problems of common interest and by employing a principle such as coduction which will enable them to do so. This implies that the challenge is also to draw upon the findings of phenomenology and linguistic analysis and to incorporate them into its program. If this is accomplished, it will mean an enrichment of behaviorism, but also a modification of its original program.

Trial Names

ROLLO HANDY and E. C. HARWOOD

A. PRELIMINARY COMMENTS

Language problems frequently impede communication in behavioral scientists' discussions of their inquiries and of the methods applied in such inquiries. This report develops a glossary of some important terms in order to diagnose some of the inconsistencies, incoherencies, or other inadequacies of language and to suggest scientific names that may prove useful to behavioral scientists.[1] Unfortunately, misunderstandings easily occur, even in the initial stages of discussion; consequently, aspects of the problem will be discussed before the trial names are suggested.

Many attempts have been made to improve naming in the behavioral sciences, and an extensive literature is concerned with definitions. In this report, no detailed attempt is made to compare our procedures with others. We begin with the framework developed by Dewey and Bentley—a framework that, it may be noted, George Lundberg was sympathetic to. In order to avoid misunderstanding, we emphasize that we are not attempting to

[1] This report relies heavily on the work of John Dewey and Arthur Bentley. See especially their *Knowing and the Known,* Boston, Beacon Press; 1949; paperback edition, 1960; and Sidney Ratner and Jules Altman, eds., *John Dewey and Arthur F. Bentley: A Philosophical Correspondence,* 1932-1951, Rutgers University Press, New Brunswick, N.J., 1964.

This report also makes use of the recent survey of the behavioral sciences by Rollo Handy and Paul Kurtz (*A Current Appraisal of the Behavioral Sciences,* Behavioral Research Council, Great Barrington, Mass., 1964).

develop or prescribe any final group of names. As Dewey and Bentley say:

> "The scientific method neither presupposes nor implies any set, rigid, theoretical position. We are too well aware of the futility of efforts to achieve greater dependability of communication and consequent mutual understanding by methods of imposition. In advancing fields of research, inquirers proceed by doing all they can to make clear to themselves and to others the points of view and the hypotheses by means of which their work is carried on." (Page V)

They further say of their approach:

> "It demands that statements be made as descriptions of events in terms of durations in time and areas in space. It excludes assertions of fixity and attempts to impose them. It installs openness and flexibility in the very process of knowing. . . . We wish the tests of openness and flexibility to be applied to our work; any attempts to impose fixity would be a denial—a rupture—of the very method we employ." (Page VI)

Our intention has been to continue the Dewey-Bentley line of advance, if it is an advance, without assuming that it necessarily is the only or even the best way to proceed. If improvement in efficiency of communication results, some progress will have been made. If instead our work impedes communication, it should be superseded by something more useful.

"Trial" is used here then, to indicate that we do not seek to fix permanently, or even standardize for a long time, the terminology suggested. Under some circumstances, standardization of terminology may have little or no scientific use. The standardization of names in alchemy or astrology, for example, would be pointless for scientific purposes (except in the sense that if all astrologers agree on the use of a particular name, refutation of their views might be easier). As scientific inquirers proceed, new similarities and differences will be discovered in the subject matter of inquiry; consequently, a fixed terminology probably would be a barrier to progress.

"Name" is used here in the Dewey-Bentley manner (See *K&K*, pp. 145 ff.), although we realize that others use that word differently. Names here are *not* regarded as things separate from, and intermediate between, the organism and its environment. Rather the focus is on naming *behavior;* on an organism-environmental transaction. Conventionally, a sharp separation has been made between a word and its so-called "meaning," but here we attempt to keep the whole naming process in view. For us, the import of "H_2O" as a scientific name is understood in relation to current scientific practices; "H_2O" is a shorthand label for certain aspects of a subject matter of inquiry, including the relations among those aspects, as observed by scientists. To concentrate on "H_2O" as a set of marks or sounds radically separated from the thing named, as some epistemologists do, is considered an undesirable separation of things that, from the viewpoint of our purpose here, usually are found together. Specifically, separation of the word, its so-called "meaning," and the word user, frequently results in hypostatization and seemingly insoluble problems of the locus and status of "meanings" and of "knowledge."

In the present context naming is the aspect of knowing with which we are concerned. Naming, as Dewey and Bentley say, "selects, discriminates, identifies, locates, orders, arranges, systematizes." (*K&K*, p. 147.)

Naming can be made "firmer," be more consistently useful, without restricting future revisions. For crude everyday purposes, naming a whale a fish may be useful; but to name it a mammal marks an improvement from the viewpoint of scientific usefulness. Revisions as to what "atom" is used to designate or name also have provided improved naming.

Our procedures in preparing this report are transactional. "Transaction" here designates or is a name for the full ongoing process in a field where all aspects and phases of the field as well as the inquirer himself are in common process. A transactional report is differentiated from self-actional reports (in which independent actors, powers, minds, etc., are assumed to function) and from interactional reports (in which presumptively independent things are found in causal interconnection). "Borrower can not borrow without lender to lend, nor lender lend without borrower to borrow, the loan being a transaction that is identifiable only in the wider transaction of the full legal-commercial system in which it is present as occurrence." (*K&K*, p. 133.)

The work and accomplishments of scientists have been described in many different ways, and no attempt is made here to settle all controversies or to endorse dogmatically any one view. Perhaps most can agree, however, that an important part of the scientist's job is the increasingly more useful description of things, including relations, that are differentiated in the cosmos.

Some authors attempt to distinguish sharply between "description" and "explanation." "Description" is used here to *include* what many refer to as "explanation," rather than in a way that contrasts a "mere" or "bare" description with a scientific "explanation." Obviously scientists seek to improve the crude descriptions of common sense, but their improved reports on their subject matter (i.e., what some label "explanations") are also descriptions in the broad sense. For example, a stick partially submerged in water appears to be bent, and a crude description may go no further than to so state. But if a more adequate description is given, in terms of light refraction, human processes of perception, human language habits, etc., then we have what is sometimes called an "explanation." The explanation of the bent appearance consists in a full description of the whole transactional process, which enables us to predict what normal human observers will see, given certain circumstances.

"Warranted assertion" is used here rather than "true statement" (or "true proposition"). "Warranted assertion" seems an appropriate name for the outcome of successful scientific inquiry. The term helps to remind us that the assertion involved is warranted by the processes of inquiry and is subject to modification or rejection by further inquiry. It also helps to exorcise the ghost that scientists have as their business the discovering of final and fixed generalizations.

As inquiry proceeds, modification of naming is to be expected. The differentiation of water from the rest of the cosmos is useful for daily life, but adopting the scientific name "H_2O" marked an improvement in that further prediction and control was facilitated. Perhaps the development of physics and chemistry will some day result in the further alteration of the naming for what in everyday life is called water.

We deny emphatically that there is any kind of intrinsic or necessary relation between the marks and sounds used in naming and what is named. In that sense, naming is wholly conventional; whether "water," "aqua," or "gkim" is used to refer to a certain liquid makes no difference. (This is not to deny, of course, that specific words are part of particular languages, and identifying "water" as a noun in the English language affords many clues as to how the word will be used by English speaking people.) On the other hand, some names are much more useful than others. "H_2O", for example, as used in current physical science, is quite different from "water" taken as designating one of the assumed four primordial elements. Although the whole notational system now used for chemical elements and their combinations is in an important sense descriptive, once the system is chosen, naming within it is determined in major respects by the system. "H_2O" as shorthand for water is not capriciously chosen but rather is the outcome of painstaking and carefully controlled inquiry. In general, then, although there is no ultimately right naming, and although all naming is conventional, scientific naming is neither capricious nor arbitrary.

Sometimes those who object that naming is too simple a process to be of much importance in scientific inquiry take a much different view of the naming process than that offered here. If strong emphasis is put on naming in relation to assertions warranted by testing, then some of those objections, at least, seem to be met. To have labels for differentiated aspects of the cosmos that have been thoroughly tested is one thing. To elaborate a terminology that stands either for aspects that have not been usefully differentiated, or for supposed aspects inconsistent with well-established "if—then" statements, is quite another matter. Perhaps both "phlogiston" and "caloric" had considerable merit as names consistently usable for various processes once assumed to occur in heat phenomena. Their deficiencies, from the present point of view, were precisely that they did not name differentiated aspects of the cosmos as found by scientific inquiry.

When those terms became entrenched in scientific discourse, however, they were not easily evicted; they were part of a semantic vested interest. Much the same almost certainly applies to many behavioral science terms now in wide and frequent use. Sometimes suggested changes in naming are rejected on the ground that new specifications (scientific namings) omit important connotations the term had in ordinary discourse or in earlier science. Here again the importance of testing can hardly be overemphasized. Rejection of "phlogiston" doubtless omitted what was once dear to many people, yet scientific progress apparently benefited from those omissions.

"Specification" is used here to refer to the naming that has been found useful in science. Specification is a different process than some of the processes frequently named "definition." "Definition" has been used to refer to such diverse things that confusion often results. As Dewey and Bentley say:

> "The one word 'definition' is expected to cover acts and products, words and things, accurate descriptions and tentative descriptions, mathematical equivalences and exact formulations, ostensive definitions, sensations and perceptions in logical report, 'ultimates,' and finally even 'indefinables.' No one word, anywhere in careful technical research, should be required to handle so many tasks." (*K&K*, p. 195.)

Broadly speaking, "definition" often is used to apply to almost any procedure for saying what the so-called "meaning" of a term is. Much of the difficulty with "definition" seems to be just its linkage with "meaning." But leaving that problem aside, a considerable variety of procedures have been used in attempts somehow to designate what a term stands for or has been applied to, and many of those procedures are highly dubious from a scientific point of view.

In this report, "specification" is used as a name for scientific naming; i.e., the efficient (especially useful) kind of designation found in modern scientific inquiry.

B. FURTHER DEVELOPMENT OF SOME BASIC NAMES

In striving for agreement on some firm, coherent, and consistent naming, proceeding initially along roughly evolutionary lines may be helpful. "Cosmos" was selected to name the sum total of the things we can see, smell, taste, hear, and feel, including relations among those things, so that we can talk about the sum total of things without repeatedly having to describe them in detail. "Cosmos" is applied to the universe as a whole system, including the speaking-naming thing who uses that name. Moreover, "cosmos" is the name for all that is included in man's knowing behavior from the most distant past discussed in scientifically warranted assertions to the probable future insofar as it is known by scientifically warranted predictions.

Next we differentiate among the vast number of things in the cosmos and select the living things; for these we choose the name "organism." Note that selecting for naming does not imply detaching the physical thing from the cosmos. Everything named remains a part of cosmos with innumerable relations to other parts.

Among the organisms, we further differentiate for the purpose of the present discussion and select for naming ourselves, our ancestors, and our progeny; these we name "man."

We then observe the transactions of man with other aspects and phases of cosmos and note the transactions named "eating," "breathing," etc. Among those numerous transactions, we differentiate further and select for naming the transactions typical of man but found infrequently or not at all in other organisms.

This type of behavior involves processes of a kind such that something stands for or is assumed to refer to something else. Such processes we name "sign behavior," or simply "sign." Note that "sign" is not the name of the thing that stands for something else; "sign," as used here, is the name of the transaction as a whole; i.e., "sign" is the short name for "sign process." For example, the word "cup" is not taken as the sign for the vessel we drink coffee from; rather the word, the container, and the word user all are regarded as aspects or phases (sometimes both) of the full situation. Sign process is the type of transaction that distinguishes some behavioral from physiological processes, a knowing behavior transaction from a transaction such as eating, digesting, seeing, etc. (But no absolute or ultimate separation is suggested; sign processes always include physiological processes and may affect those processes, as when the reading of a telegram containing bad news affects respiration.)

Sign process in evolutionary development has progressed through the following still-existing stages:

a. The signaling or perceptive-manipulative stage of sign in transactions such as beckoning, whistling, frowning, etc.

b. The naming stage as used generally in speaking and writing.

c. The symboling stage as used in symbolic logic and mathematics.

Focusing our attention now on the naming stage of sign process, we choose to name it "designation." Designation always is behavior, an organism-environmental transaction typical primarily, if not exclusively, of man in the cosmos. Designation includes:

1. The earliest stage of designation or naming in the evolutionary scale, which we shall name "cue."

> "By Cue is to be understood the most primitive language-behavior. ... Cue, as primitive naming, is so close to the situation of its origin that at time it enters almost as if a signal itself. Face-to-face perceptive situations are characteristic of its type of locus. It may include cry, expletive, or other single-word sentences, or any onomatopoeic utterance; and in fully developed language it may appear as an interjection, exclamation, abbreviated utterance, or other casually practical communicative convenience." (*K&K,* pp. 156-7.)

2. A more advanced level of designation or naming in the evolutionary scale, which we shall name "characterization." This name applies to the everyday use of words; usage that is reasonably adequate for many practical purposes of life.

3. For the, at present, farthest advanced level of designation we use "specification." This name applies to the highly developed naming behavior best exhibited in modern scientific inquiry.

For the purpose of economizing words in discourse, we need a general name for the bits and pieces of cosmos differentiated and named. For this general name we choose "fact." Fact is the name for cosmos in course of being known through naming by man (with man included among the aspects of cosmos) in a statement sufficiently developed to exhibit temporal and spatial localizations. Fact includes all namings-named durationally and extensionally spread; it is not limited to what is known to, and named by, any one man at any moment or even in his life time.

Frequently, we have need to discuss a limited range of fact where our attention is focused for the time being. For this we choose the name "situation." This is the blanket name for those facts localized in time and space for our immediate attention.

Within a situation we frequently have occasion to refer to durational changes among facts. For these we choose the name "events."

Finally, in discussing events we usually have occasion to refer to aspects of the fact involved that are least vague or more firmly determined and more accurately specified. For those we choose the name "object." Object is differentiated from event in being more accurately specified; it is an aspect of the subject matter of inquiry insofar as it has reached an orderly and settled form.

Further tentative comments on sign process may be helpful. The transition from sign process at the perceptive-manipulative stage (here designated "signaling") to the initial naming stage (designated "cueing") is a change from the simplest attention-getting procedures, by evolutionary stages, to a somewhat more complex sign process that begins to describe things and events.

No clear line of demarcation is found. Some perceptive-manipulative signalings as well as primitive word cues are more descriptive than they are simple alerting behavior.

The transition from cueing to characterizing also reflects evolutionary development with increasing complexity of process, including formal grammar, etc.

And the further transition from characterizing to specifying in the manner of modern science reflects the further evolutionary development of sign process, a still more complicated procedure.

At first thought the stage we have here designated "symboling" may seem to be a marked departure from, or to reflect a break in, the evolutionary development of sign process. However, mathematical symboling, at least as frequently used in scientific inquiry, may be considered shorthand specifying. Each symbol replaces one or more words. A single mathematical equation may replace a long and involved sentence, even a paragraph, or a longer description in words.

Sometimes symboling is considered to be different from naming, and even Dewey and Bentley speak of its as an "advance of sign beyond naming, accompanied by disappearance of specific reference such as naming develops." (*K&k,* p. 303.) Mathematical inquiry seems in some respects to differ in kind from the designation used in empirical inquiry, yet the mathematical symbols used in scientific inquiry designate something quite specific; equivalences or other relations, for example. For the purposes of empirical inquiry, aspects of the formal mathematical structure are used to facilitate summarizing and focusing attention on relations among things.

Thus sign process in its evolutionary progress to date may be described as the efforts of man to communicate: first by simple perceptive-manipulative processes; then by verbal processes of increasing complexity, until this increasing complexity of verbal procedure became so much of a barrier to further progress that a shorthand system was devised in order to facilitate further communication. This shorthand system has been most extensively developed in mathematical symboling.

C. LIST OF TRIAL NAMES

Many of the names below were taken from Ch. II of Dewey and Bentley's *Knowing and the Known,* while others were used in *A Current Appraisal of the Behavioral Sciences.* The importance of the names does not stem from their sources, but rather from their aid in facilitating communication. The names below are provisionally claimed to be important in the sense that we found them useful in trying to communicate more successfully among ourselves. (In some instances, the names are listed because we found them to be barriers to mutual understanding.) However, other names overlooked by us may prove to be even more useful than those we here discuss, and some of those presently regarded as useful may prove to be grossly misleading on further inquiry.

A final suggestion to the reader: The prevalence of interactional and self-actional theoretical assumptions may make the transactional approach unfamiliar at first sight. With reference to nomenclature, what seems obvious in self-actional or interactional terms frequently is deficient from a transactional point of view.[2] What may seem odd, peculiar, or overly simple—judged in terms of an acceptance of other frameworks—becomes useful, appropriate, and sometimes necessary, given the transactional approach.

For example, Dewey and Bentley have been severely criticized for neglecting what the critics regard as obvious and necessary for all work in the field: distinguishing radically between psychology and logic. Their reply follows:

> "We may assure all such critics that from early youth we have been aware of an *academic* and *pedagogical* distinction of logical from psychological. We certainly make no attempt to deny it, and

[2] The prevalence of nontransactional behavior in inquiry reflects linguistic habits not easily changed. For example, although the authors of *A Current Appraisal of the Behavioral Sciences* adopted a transactional method, they sometimes inadvertently separated "internal"–"external," "individual"–"social," "organism"–"environment," and a word from its so-called "meaning," with resulting incoherence. The discussion in the glossary section of the present report suggests the dangers of fusing "biological" and "physiological," and helps to point out the lack of clarity in some of the uses of "operational" and "specification."

we do not disregard it. Quite the contrary. Facing this distinction in the presence of actual life processes and behaviors of human beings, we deny any rigid *factual* difference such as the academic treatment implies.... We have as strong an objection to the assumption of a science of psychology severed from a logic and yet held basic to that logic, as we have to a logic severed from a psychology and proclaimed as if it existed in a realm of its own where it regards itself as basic to the psychology. *We regard knowings and reasonings and mathematical and scientific adventurings even up to their highest abstractions, as activities of men—as veritably men's behaviors*—and we regard the study of these particular knowing behaviors as lying within the general field of behavioral inquiry..." (*K&K,* pp. 308-9; Emphasis in last sentence not in original.)

Note: In the entries below, some quotations are taken from *Knowing and the Known,* Ch. 11. Unless otherwise indicated, we agree with the material quoted.

ACCURATE: Dewey and Bentley suggest this adjective to "characterize degrees of achievement" in the range of specification. However, "degrees of achievement" seems to imply some standards of comparison; standards that we do not have. We suggest that names in the range of scientific specification may be more or less accurate in the sense of more or less painstakingly chosen and applied. Perhaps Dewey and Bentley were naming the same characteristics of naming behavior by their phrase "degrees of achievement." We suggest that "accurate" be used as a short name for "to date found most useful scientifically or by scientists." See PRECISE.

ACTION, ACTIVITY: These words are used here only to characterize loosely durational-extensional subject matters of inquiry. The words suggest self-actional or interactional assumptions in which actions are the doings of independent selves, minds, etc., separated from the full organism-environmental transaction; approaches that are rejected here for inquiry into knowings-known. See INTERACTION; SELF-ACTION; BEHAVIOR.

ACTOR: A confusing although widely used word. "Actor" often is used in ways that unfortunately separate the doer too sharply from the complex behavioral transaction. "Actor" here is used only in the sense of "Trans-actor," the human aspect of a behavioral situation.

APPLICATION: In the terminology adopted here, a name is said to be *applied* to the thing named. Use of "application" helps to avoid the connotation of some intrinsic or necessary relation between the thing named and the marks or sounds used in naming.

ASPECT: The name for any differentiated part of a full transaction, without special durational stress. (For the latter see PHASE.) The aspects are not taken as independent "reals." In a borrower-lender transaction, the borrower, the lender, and what is lent are among the aspects of the transaction. Those aspects are inseparable in that there is no borrowing without lending, and vice-versa.

BEHAVIOR: The name here covers all the adjustmental processes of organism-in-environment. This differs from other uses that limit "behavior" to the muscular and glandular actions of organisms in "purposive" processes, or to the "external" rather than "internal" processes of the organism. "Behavior" here is always used transactionally, never as of the organism alone, but instead as of the organism-environmental process. (This is not to deny that *provisional* separation of organism and environment, within a transactional framework, can be useful in inquiry.)

BEHAVIORISM: Although many conflicting behaviorist approaches can be found, a common feature is the rejection of traditional mentalistic and introspective approaches to human behavior. We agree that the latter should be rejected. However, care should be taken to distinguish our transactional approach from many types of behaviorism, because some behaviorists regard behavior as occurring strictly within the organism or regard behavior as physiological. Our rejection of traditional presuppositions should not be understood as implying exclusion of physiological processes within a brain; we include them as aspects of sign behavior. (See SIGN BEHAVIOR; TRANSACTION.)

BIOLOGICAL: The name given here to those processes in living organisms that are not currently explorable by the techniques of the physical sciences alone. Biological inquiry covers inquiry into both physiological and sign-behavior. No ultimate separation between the physical and biological "realms" is assumed, nor do we assume that present physical and physiological techniques of inquiry will remain unchanged. Perhaps future inquiry will make our present divisions of subject matters unsuitable. See PHYSICAL.

CHARACTERIZATION: This name is applied to the everyday use of words that is reasonably adequate for many practical purposes. Characterization is a more advanced stage of designation than cueing, but less advanced than specifying.

CIRCULARITY: In self-actional and interactional framework, circular procedures may constitute grievous faults. In explicitly transactional inquiry, some circularity is to be expected. For example, the methodological framework of a transactional approach reflects observation of scientists conducting inquiries, and the resulting framework is used to improve efficiency of observation. Some critics of Dewey and Bentley regard the type of circularity found in *Knowing and the Known* as a major flaw, but they apparently fail to grasp the significance of the Dewey-Bentley procedures.

CONCEPT, CONCEPTION: "Concept" is used in so many ways, especially in mentalistic and hypostatized forms, and in ways separating the sign from the sign-user, that its total avoidance is here recommended. "Conception" is frequently construed as a "mentalistic entity," but sometimes as a synonym for a point of view provisionally held and to be inquired into. Even in the latter instance, the word may have mentalistic connotations. We are convinced that it is not useful because it so often is a semantic trap for the unwary.

COHERENCE: The word is applied by us not to the internal consistency of a set of symbols, but to the connection found in scientific inquiry to obtain between or among objects. Not logical connection, then, but the kind of "hanging together" that occurs in observed regularities, is what is named.

CONNECTION: In naming-knowing transactions, the general name for the linkages among the aspects of a process, as found through inquiry. In an observed regularity, the things involved in the regularity are said to be connected. "Connection" covers the relations sometimes referred to as "causal," "statistical," "probabalistic," "structural-functional," etc.

CONSCIOUSNESS: Not used by us unless as a synonym for "awareness".

CONSISTENCY: Discourse found to be free of contradictory and of contrary assertions is characterized as consistent.

CONTEXT: Here used transactionally to refer to the mutually related circumstances and conditions under which things (objects and events) are observed.

COSMOS: Names the sum total of things we can see, smell, taste, hear, and feel, including relations among those things. "Cosmos" is applied to the universe as a whole system, including the speaking-naming thing who uses the name "cosmos." The time range involved stretches from the earliest of events scientifically known to the future events scientifically predictable (e.g. path of a comet). Not to be construed as something underlying knowing-knowns yet itself unknowable.

CUE: The earliest stage of designation or naming in the evolutionary scale. Primitive naming, here called "cueing," is close to signaling, and no clear line of demarcation between them is found. The differentiation is made on the basis that organized language occurs in cueing. Some psychologists use "cue" for what we name "signal," and vice-versa. If such psychological use develops firmly, our use will be superseded.

DEFINITION: Often used in a broad sense to cover any procedure for indicating the "meaning" of a term, including: the stipulation of the use of a term in technical contexts (as when "ohm" is chosen as the name for a unit of electrical resistance); descriptions of the uses a term has in everyday speech; equations relating a single symbol and a combination of symbols for which the single symbol is an abbreviation (as in symbolic logic); what is here called "specification"; as well as many other procedures. Also used to refer to a description of the "nature" or "essence" of a thing. In view of the many widely varying procedures "definition" has been used to name, we avoid the term here. See SPECIFICATION.

DESCRIPTION: Expansion of naming or designation in order to communicate about things (including situations, events, objects, and relations) on which attention is focused.

DESIGNATION: Always considered here transactionally as behavior. Includes cueing, characterizing, and specifying. When naming and named are viewed in common process, "designation" refers to the naming aspect of the transaction. Designation is the knowing-naming *aspect* of fact.

ENTITY: Its use often presupposes a self-actional or interactional framework, and especially some independent-of-all-else kind of existence. Not used here. See THING.

ENVIRONMENT: *Not* considered here as something surrounding, and fully separable from organisms; but as one aspect of organism-environmental transactions. The apparently plausible separation of organism from environment breaks down when one attempts to locate and consistently describe the exact demarcation between organism and environment. For some purposes of inquiry, focusing attention primarily on either the organic or the environmental aspect of the whole transaction may be useful.

EPISTEMOLOGICAL: To the extent the use of "epistemological" supposes that knowers and knowns are fully separable the word is incompatible with transactional procedures and is not used here.

EVENT: The name chosen here for durational changes among facts upon which attention is focused for purposes of inquiry.

EXACT: See PRECISE, ACCURATE.

EXCITATION: To be used in reference to physiological organism-environmental processes when differentiation between such physiological stimulation and sign-behavioral stimulation is desired. See STIMULUS.

EXISTENCE: The known-named aspect of fact. Physical, physiological, and behavioral subject matters are regarded here as equally existing. However, "existence" should not be considered as referring to any "reality" supposedly supporting the known but itself unknowable.

EXPERIENCE: "This word has two radically opposed uses in current discussion. These overlap and shift so as to cause continual confusion and unintentional misrepresentation. One stands for short extensive-durational process, an extreme form of which is identification of an isolated sensory event or 'sensation' as an ultimate unit of inquiry. The other covers the entire spatially extensive, temporally durational application; and here it is a counterpart for the word 'cosmos'." "Experience" sometimes is used to name something considered to be primarily localized in the organism ("he experienced delight") or to what includes much beyond the organism ("the experience of the nation at war"); to relatively short durational-extensional processes ("he experienced a twinge") and to relatively vast processes ("the experience of the race"). "The word 'experience' should be dropped entirely from discussion unless held strictly to a single definite use: that, namely, of calling attention to the fact that *Existence* has organism and environment as its aspects, and cannot be identified with either as an independent isolate." See BEHAVIOR.

FACT: The cosmos in course of being known through naming by organisms, themselves being always among its aspects. Fact is the general name for bits and pieces of cosmos as known through naming, in a statement sufficiently developed to exhibit temporal and spatial localizations. (Man is included among the aspects of cosmos.) "It is knowings-knowns, durationally and extensionally spread; not what is known to and named by any one organism in any passing moment, nor to any one organism in its lifetime. Fact is under way among organisms advancing in a cosmos, itself under advance as known. The word 'fact,' etymologically from *factum*, something done, with its temporal implications, is much better fitted for the broad use here suggested than for either of its extreme and less common, though more pretentious applications: on the one hand for an independent 'real'; on the other for a 'mentally' endorsed report."

FIELD: "On physical analogies this word should have important application in behavioral inquiry. The physicist's uses, however, are still undergoing reconstructions, and the definite correspondence needed for behavioral application can not be established. Too many current projects for the use of the word have been parasitic.

Thorough transactional studies of behaviors on their own account are needed to establish behavioral field in its own right." "Field" here names a cluster of connected facts as found in inquiry. We do not use "field" as the name for a presumed separate environment in which independent facts are found; "field" names the entire complex process of mutually connected things and their relations on which attention is focused, and includes the observer in the transaction.

FIRM: Namings are firm to the extent that they are found to be useful for consistent and coherent communication about things, including events. Firmness, thus demonstrated, involves no implication of finality or of immunity to being superseded as scientific inquiry advances.

HUMAN: The word used to differentiate ourselves, our ancestors, and our progeny from the remainder of the cosmos. No ultimate division of the cosmos into man, other organisms, and physical objects is intended. Nor, obviously, do we intend by our naming to deny man's evolutionary development from other organisms, or the myriad connections man has with other aspects of the cosmos.

IDEA, IDEAL: "Underlying differences of employment are so many and wide that, where these words are used, it should be made clear whether they are used behaviorally or as names of presumed existences taken to be strictly mental." "Idea" may be serviceable as referring to a notion about things.

INDIVIDUAL: "Abandonment of this word and of all substitutes for it seems essential wherever a positive *general theory* is undertaken or planned. Minor specialized studies in individualized phrasing should expressly name the limits of the application of the word, and beyond that should hold themselves firmly within such limits." In the transactional framework here adopted, "behavior" covers both so-called "individual" and "social" behavior, which are aspects of behavioral transactions. See BEHAVIOR.

INQUIRY: "A strictly transactional name. It is an equivalent of knowing, but preferable as a name because of its freedom from 'mentalistic' associations." Scientific inquiry is the attempt to develop ever more accurate descriptions (including what are often called "explanations") of the things and their relations that are differentiated in cosmos, in order to facilitate prediction and control (or adjustive behavior thereto). Statements about the observed regularities, measurements of change, etc., are formulated as warranted assertions. Transactionally viewed, inquiry is a phase of knowing behavior.

INTER: "This prefix has two sets of applications (see Oxford Dictionary). One is for 'between,' 'in-between,' or 'between the parts of.' The other is for 'mutually,' 'reciprocally.' " (E.g., this prefix sometimes is applied to the relation "in-between," as when mind and body are said to interact in the pineal gland, or that a tennis ball is intermediate in size between a golf ball and a soft ball. Sometimes "inter" is used for mutually reciprocal relations, as in the interaction of hunter and hunted.) "The result of this shifting use as it enters philosophy, logic, and psychology, no matter how inadvertent, is ambiguity and undependability." The habit of mingling without clarification the two sets of implications is easily acquired; we use "inter" for instances in which the "in-between" sense is dominant, and the prefix "trans" is used where mutually reciprocal influence is included.

INTERACTION: "This word, because of its prefix, is undoubtedly the source of much of the more serious difficulty in discussion at the present time." Some authors use "interaction" in the way "transaction" is used here. We restrict "interaction" to instances in which presumptively independent things are balanced against each other in causal interconnection, as in Newtonian mechanics. For inquiry into knowing-knowns, such an interactional approach is rejected. See TRANSACTION.

KNOWINGS: Organic aspects of transactionally observed behaviors. Here considered in the familiar central range of namings-knowings.

KNOWLEDGE: "In current employment this word is too wide and vague to be a *name* of anything in particular. The butterfly 'knows' how to mate, presumably without learning; the dog 'knows' its master through learning; man 'knows' through learning how to do an immense number of things in the way of arts or abilities; he also 'knows' physics, and 'knows' mathematics; he knows *that, what,* and *how.* It should require only a moderate acquaintance with philosophical literature to observe that the vagueness and ambiguity of the word 'knowledge' accounts for a large number of the traditional 'problems' called *the problem of knowledge.* The issues that must be faced before firm use is gained are: Does the word 'knowledge' indicate something the organism possesses or produces? Or does it indicate something the organism confronts or with which it comes into contact? Can either of these viewpoints be coherently maintained? If not, what change in preliminary description must be sought?" See WARRANTED ASSERTION.

KNOWNS: "Known" refers to one aspect of transactionally observed behaviors, i.e., to what is named. "In the case of namings-knowings the range of the knowns is that of existence within fact or cosmos, not in a limitation to the recognized affirmations of the moment, but in process of advance in long durations."

LANGUAGE: Here viewed transactionally as behavior of men (with the possibility open that inquiry may show that other organisms also exhibit language behavior). Word-users here are not split from word-meanings, nor word-meanings from words.

MANIPULATION: See PERCEPTION-MANIPULATION.

MATTER, MATERIAL: See PHYSICAL. If the word "mental" is dropped, the word "material" (in the sense of matter as opposed to mind) falls out also.

MATHEMATICS: Here regarded as a behavior developing out of naming activities and specializing in symboling, or shorthand naming. See SYMBOLING.

MEANING: Not used here, because of confusion engendered by past and current uses. The transactional approach rejects the split between bodies-devoid-of-meaning and disembodied meanings.

MENTAL: Not used here. Its use typically reflects the hypostatization of one aspect of sign behavior.

NAME, NAMING, NAMED: Naming is here regarded as a form of knowing. Names are *not* considered here as third things separate from and intermediate between the organism and its environment. Naming transactions are language behavior in its central ranges.

Naming states, selects, identifies, orders, systematizes, etc. We at times use "designating" as a synonym for "naming."

OBJECT: Within fact, and within its existential phase, object is that which has been most firmly specified, and is thus distinguished from situation and event. Object is an aspect of situation inquired into insofar as useful description or firm naming of that aspect has been achieved.

OBJECTIVE: Used here only in the sense of "impartial" or "unbiased."

OBSERVATION: Used here transactionally, rather than as a separated "activity" either of the observer or the observed. Observation and reports upon it are regarded as tentative and hypothetical. Observation is not limited to "sense-perception" in the narrow sense; i.e., to a "simple" sensory quality or some other supposed "content" of such short time-span as to have no or few connections. Observation refers to what is accessible and attainable publicly. Both knowings and electrons, for example, are taken as being as observable as trees or chairs.

OPERATION: "The word 'operation' as applied to behavior in recent methodological discussions should be thoroughly overhauled and given the full transactional status that such words as 'process' and 'activity' require. The military use of the word is suggestive of the way to deal with it."

OPERATIONISM: This has become a confusing word, and sometimes seems to be merely an invocation of scientific virtue. "Operational definition" sometimes refers to defining phrases having an "if—then" form ("x is water soluble"="if x is immersed in water, then it dissolves"); sometimes to the insistence that the criteria of application of a word be expressed in terms of experimental procedures; and sometimes to a statement of the observable objects and events that are covered in the use of a word. On some occasions, "operational definition" apparently is used to refer to something similar to, if not identical with, what we call "specification" or scientific naming. See SPECIFICATION.

ORGANISM: Used here to differentiate living things from other things in the cosmos, but *not* to detach organisms from their many connections with other aspects of cosmos. Organisms are selected for separate naming for methodological purposes, not as constituting something separated from the rest of cosmos.

PERCEPT: In the transactional framework, a percept is regarded as an aspect of signaling behavior, not as a hypostatized independent something.

PERCEPTION-MANIPULATION: Although perception and manipulation are regarded as radically different in some theoretical frameworks, transactionally viewed they have a common behavioral status. They occur jointly and inseparably in the range of what is here called signal behavior.

PHENOMENON: Used here for provisional identification of situations. Not to be construed as "subjective," nor as a mere appearance of an underlying reality.

PHASE: Used for an aspect of cosmos when attention is focused on the duration of a relative time sequence, as when referring to the various phases of the manufacture and distribution of products.

PHYSICAL: At present, we find three major divisions of subject matter of inquiry: physical, physiological, and sign-behavioral. These divisions are made on the basis of present techniques of inquiry, not on the basis of assumed essential differences. See BIOLOGICAL.

PHYSIOLOGICAL: "That portion of biological inquiry which forms the second outstanding division of the subjectmatter of all inquiry as at present in process; differentiated from the physical by the techniques of inquiry employed more significantly than by mention of its specialized organic locus." See BEHAVIORISM.

PRECISE: Dewey and Bentley use "exact" as an adjective to describe symbols, and "accurate" to describe specifying. We question the usefulness of differentiating between specifying and symboling other than to point out that the latter seems to be shorthand for the former. Because symbols are often used in connection with relatively precise measurements for the purposes of scientific inquiry, we suggest that "precise" may be more useful than "exact" as an adjective characterizing any symbolizing. Symbols are precise to the extent that they are shorthand names for precise measurements or what could be precise measurements. See ACCURATE.

PROCESS: To be used aspectually or phasally as naming a series of related events.

PROPOSITION: Used sometimes in the context of logic to name the states-of-affairs to which statements (or assertions, or sentences) refer. Thus "The dog is black" and "Der Hund ist schwarz" are said to express the same proposition. Generally such procedures make sharp distinctions among words, word-users, and "meanings," or among namers, nameds, and names. Such separations are here rejected, and along with them go many related distinctions. We regard the talkings (including namings, thinkings, reasonings, etc.) of man as human behavior rather than as third things somehow occurring between men and what they talk about, and we believe that proceeding in this manner not only avoids many needless mysteries but aids scientific inquiry into such talkings.

QUEST FOR CERTAINTY: In prescientific inquiry, the attempt to discover an eternal and immutable "reality" that can be known with complete certainty. We do not assert the absolute nonexistence of such "reality," but point out the failure to find it and the barrier such a notion has been to scientific progress. In somewhat disguised forms, the quest for certainty crops up in purportedly scientific investigations, as in attempts to find a certain and indubitable base upon which inquiry rests.

REACTION: In physiological stimulation (as contrasted with sign-behavioral stimulation), "excitation" and "reaction" are coupled as aspects of the stimulation transaction. See EXCITATION, STIMULUS.

REAL: Used sparingly as a synonym for "genuine," in opposition to "sham" or "counterfeit."

REALITY: "As commonly used, it may rank as the most metaphysical of all words in the most obnoxious sense of metaphysics, since it is supposed to name something which lies underneath and behind all knowing, and yet, as Reality, something incapable of being known in fact and as fact."

RESPONSE: In signaling behavior, as differentiated from physiological stimulation, "stimulus" and "response" are coupled as aspects of the stimulation transaction.

SCIENCE, SCIENTIFIC: "Our use of this word is to designate the most advanced stage of specification of our times—the 'best knowledge' by the tests of employment and indicated growth."

SELF: Within the framework here adopted, "self" names one aspect of organism-environmental transactions, rather than an hypostatized "entity."

SELF-ACTION: "Used to indicate various primitive treatments of the known, prior in historical development to interactional and transactional treatments." That is, used to refer to frameworks in which presumptively independent actors, minds, selves, etc., are viewed as causing events (as, for example, when gods are said to cause meteorological phenomena, or minds to create new ideas). "Rarely found today except in philosophical, logical, epistemological, and a few limited psychological regions of inquiry."

SIGN: The name used here to name organism-environmental transactions in which the organism involved in a situation accepts one thing as a reference or pointing to some other thing. "Sign" here is *not* the name of the thing that is taken as referring to something else; rather "sign" names the whole transaction. The evolutionary stages of "sign" are here named "signal," "name," and "symbol."

SIGNAL: Used here to refer to the perceptive-manipulative stage of sign process in transactions such as beckoning, whistling, frowning, etc. No clear line of demarcation between signaling and cueing is found; some perceptive-manipulative signalings are not only alerting behaviors, but also may begin to describe aspects of cosmos.

SIGN-BEHAVIOR: Sign-behavior refers to that range of biological inquiry in which the processes studied are not currently explorable by physical or physiological techniques alone. Human behavior here covers both so-called "social" and "individual" behavior. No "ultimate" separation of physical, physiological, and sign-behavior is assumed; the distinction made here concerns the techniques of inquiry found useful for various types of subject-matters. See PHYSICAL, PHYSIOLOGICAL.

SIGN-PROCESS: Synonym for SIGN.

SITUATION: Used here as a blanket name for a limited range of fact, localized in time and space, upon which attention is focused. "In our transactional development, the word is not used in the sense of environment; if so used, it should not be allowed to introduce transactional implications tacitly."

SOCIAL: See INDIVIDUAL.

SPACE-TIME: Space and time are here used transactionally and behaviorally, rather than as fixed, given frames (formal, absolute, or Newtonian) or physical somethings. Bentley's words suggest our present approach: "The behaviors are present events conveying pasts into futures. They cannot be reduced to successions of instants nor to successions of locations. They themselves span extension and duration. The pasts and the futures are rather phases of behavior than its control."[3]

SPECIFICATION: Used here to refer to the naming that has been found useful in science. "The most highly perfected naming behavior. Best exhibited in modern science. Requires freedom from the defectively realistic application of the form of syllogism commonly known as Aristotelian." Should *not* be mistaken as a synonym for "definition," at least in many senses of the latter word.

STIMULUS: Used in various ways in current inquiry, sometimes designating an object or group of objects in the environment, sometimes something in the organism (events in the receptors, for example), and sometimes something located elsewhere. The near chaos connected with this word strongly suggests the need for a transactional approach. "Stimulation" may be a preferable term, inasmuch as it suggests a transactional process.

SUBJECT: Used here in the sense of "topics," as in "subjectmatter being inquired into," rather than in any sense postulating a radical separation of subject and object.

[3] Arthur F. Bentley, *Inquiry Into Inquiries* (Sidney Ratner, ed.) Boston, Beacon Press, 1954, p. 222.

SUBJECTIVE: The usual subjective-objective dichotomy is rejected here, and what commonly are called "subject" and "object" are regarded as aspects of relevant transactions. However, inasmuch as some inquiries in philosophy and psychology still use procedures based on "subjective" analysis or introspection, we emphasize our objection to whatever is not publicly observable. Subjectivism, understood as a procedure of inquiry attempting to obtain scientifically useful "knowledge" from what is not publicly accessible, is rejected here.

SUBJECTMATTER: "Whatever is before inquiry where inquiry has the range of namings-named. The main divisions in present-day research are into physical, physiological, and behavioral."

SUBSTANCE: No word of this type has a place in the present system of naming.

SYMBOL: A shorthand naming component of symboling behavior. As used here, not to be hypostatized, but viewed transactionally and comparable with "name" and "signal."

SYMBOLING: Symboling, in scientific inquiry, is a shorthand means of specifying or scientifically naming. In the development of pure mathematics structures, consistency within the symbol system is of primary importance. In such instances the symbols do not directly designate specific things and events but rather designate potential relations. (E.g., "2" does not name the type of thing that "dog" does.) However, when mathematics is used in scientific inquiry, the mathematical symbols are applied to the subject matter; then the symbols become shorthand specifications or abbreviated names.

SYSTEM: Used here as a blanket name to refer to sets or assemblages or things associated together and viewed as a whole. Systems may be self-actional, interactional, or transactional. Typically used here in the transactional sense of "full-system," in which the components or aspects are not viewed as separate things except provisionally and for special purposes other than a full report on the whole situation.

TERM: "This word has today accurate use as a name only in mathematical formulation where, even permitting it several different applications, no confusion results. The phrase 'in terms of' is often convenient and, simply used, is harmless. In the older syllogism term long retained a surface appearance of exactness which it lost when the language-existence issues involved became too prominent. For the most part in current writing it seems to be used loosely for 'word carefully employed.' It is, however, frequently entangled in the difficulties of concept. Given sufficient agreement among workers, term could perhaps be safely used for the range of specification, and this without complications arising from its mathematical uses."

THING: Used here as the general name for whatever is named. Things include both objects and events; any and every aspect of cosmos.

TIME: See SPACE-TIME.

TRANS: This prefix is used to indicate mutually reciprocal relations. See INTER.

TRANSACTION: Refers here to the full ongoing process in a field. In knowing-naming transactions, the connections among aspects of the field and the inquirer himself are in common process. To be distinguished from "interaction" and "self-action." SEE INTERACTION and SELF-ACTION.

TRUE, TRUTH: The many conflicting uses of these words incline us not to use them. In their senses of "can be relied upon," "in accordance with states-of-affairs," and "conformable to fact," they name what we call "warranted assertions." However, the connotation of permanence, fixity, and immutability suggests the quest for certainty. See WARRANTED ASSERTION.

VAGUE: This term refers to various types of inaccuracy and imprecision. Probably "vagueness" could profitably be replaced by other words indicating just what type of inaccuracy or imprecision is involved.

WARRANTED ASSERTION: Used here to refer to those assertions best certified by scientific inquiry. Such assertions are open to future correction, modification, and rejection; no finality is attributed to them. See INQUIRY.

WORD: As used here, there is no supposed separation of "meaning" from a physical vehicle somehow carrying that "meaning." Words are viewed transactionally as an aspect of knowing behavior; the subject matter is inquired into whole, as it comes, not as bifurcated.

Overtures to a New Curriculum and Research Program

ALFRED de GRAZIA

From his earliest beginnings and in every setting, man has buried gifts with the departed. In character, the gifts have ranged from a hot meal to an eternal diamond. The vain intelligentsia of modern days have taken it upon themselves to commemorate death with their deathless prose.

A tough-minded behavioralist with a sense of humor, George Lundberg would probably grin at this practice. He had a keen sense for the superstitious. Our academic foibles were plain to him. He might be expected furthermore to add that the modern "information explosion" is indeed an artificial Vesuvius, built so as to bury the very people who built it so as not to die.

I may not evade the irony. So I offer in memoriam something tentative, pieces that lay no claim to finality or even duration: behavioral science in process. It is a hot meal, not an eternal diamond. I think, too, that he might appreciate a little of this among the more durable offerings. Certainly no one would know better than he, with his pragmatic philosophy and sociology of science, that very often the important communications among scientists on a subject are completed before its final encapsulation in a form that is commonly considered to be "publication." Verification of this hypothesis has come recently through the studies by an American Psychological Association team of the informal distribution of research work and findings before their appearance in journals or books.

From the files, therefore, I have selected two recent manuscripts that represent everyday objects of our age, whose existence is fugitive and informal. One is an abstract of remarks from a lecture on the curriculum of political science. The other is of the genus of proposals to foundations.

I. THE IDEAL CURRICULUM IN POLITICAL SCIENCE[1]

I said that I would deal with the curriculum of political science, and so I shall, talking first of the curriculum for the third and fourth year of college.

Now newly appointed to the faculty of Red River University (it used to be called Red River State Teacher's College, but is now a glass and stone mushroom of the University of California), we wonder what in the world we should teach to the hundreds of students who wish to major in political science. (Any resemblance between what we propose and the program of our own University, I trust you will observe, is strictly coincidental.)

We decide right off that we shall be very broad and shall build them up gradually for the awful descriptive detail that must come soon or later in our discipline.

And first of all we would probably give them a course on "POWER" in all its manifestations. Especially its manifestations in the state. For that we should probably use a book such as Charles Merriam's *Political Power*.[2] Power should be analyzed also as a factor in the government of universities, of labor unions, of churches, and of other groups, as well as of government in particular. You may think that this is an old established sort of treatment,

[1] Extract of remarks from a lecture to a hundred students in the course "The Scope of Political Science," G53.1000, November, 1966 (smiles and groans omitted).

[2] Only a few works and writers were mentioned in the talk. They are intended to give the flavor of the courses. A formal list of 200 recommended works is in preparation.

but still 80% of the Departments of Political Science in the country would look at you aghast if you suggested that political science be the study of power in all of its manifestations.

However, you pluckily move along; you have not yet become bureaucratized, and suggest a set of courses to which you attach the label "political" but which deal really with the realm of the social sciences other than politics. Hence you suggest that there be a course on "POLITICAL ANTHROPOLOGY." And this course on political anthropology would deal not only with the present day primitive tribes but with the origins of politics and would concern itself with works such as Sigmund Freud's *Totem and Taboo.* Is it true that authority originally consisted in the father of the horde, and that the brothers, when the father got weak enough, disposed of him and ate him? And that they introjected this cannibalism into their own souls and ever since have felt guilty about authority, etc.

Now you are really waking up your students with this course in political anthropology, and you give them Kluckholm's *Mirror for Man* to read. It is a fascinating as well as authoritative textbook in anthropology. Perhaps also some work such as Pritchard's on African governments.

Then you would ask them to take a course on "POLITICAL GEOGRAPHY." There you would perhaps again introduce them to a standard work in the field from the geographer's standpoint. H. N. Ginsburg's *Atlas of Economic Development,* sets forth all the dimensions that the human geographer takes into account today. But also essays such as Nicholas Spykman's *Geography of the Peace* convey the idea that a large part of this discipline can be viewed from the standpoint of political science. You might give them some book on population problems; Philip Hauser's clear little book of a couple of years ago on that subject would do well.

And now who would be teaching all of this? As the junior teacher in the department, *you* would be. It would be one of several courses that you would be charged with. However, this would be an improvement from the day when a young college teacher had to teach seven or eight courses, sandwiched between advising students and managing the band, coaching the hockey team, and so on. But you will find another bright "interdisciplene" from anthropology or geography, and he would agree to help you teach the course, if you would put in appearances in his, until you both achieved tenure status and could insist that the budget include each of you in the other capacity. Improvise!

Then you would prescribe a course in "POLITICAL SOCIOLOGY." You might assign a work such as Robert McIver's *Web of Government.* Also useful would be Robin Williams' *American Society,* or Edward Banfield's *Political Influence,* which is about public opinion, political movements and elites engaged in solving the problems of the modern city.

You would go on to a course in "POLITICAL ECONOMY" where you would employ works such as Shumpeter's *Capitalism, Socialism and Democracy.* I was reading Arthur Schlesinger, Jr.'s *The Vital Center* last week (I won't describe it to you or even recommend it to you. It is rather humdrum history and journalism. It's not one of your lifetime's capacity of two thousand books, so far as I am concerned. But I had a special reason for reading it. Sort of paid to do it.) There Schlesinger expresses his philosophy which is not liberalism—well, it is liberalism,—well, you know, it *is* liberalism and it's *not* liberalism, it is socialism and isn't socialism, it's definitely not fascism nor is it communism, in fact he is very anti-fascist to begin with and he gets more and more anti-communist as he goes along. Anyway, he reproaches Schumpeter in the new foreword of 1962, written when he had tasted the fruits of power, for having made him think too badly of the American businessman. It seems that in 1949 when he first wrote the book, he had been still under the influence of Schumpeter, who taught at Harvard and was sure that capitalism was going down the drain. So he favored socialism. But Schumpeter was a fine economist and would not necessarily be so corruptive of such hardened New York capitalists as you all are.

You might find more readable books too. I think of Richard Tawney's *The Acquisitive Society* or Thorstein Veblen's *The Engineers and the Price System,* but don't like the philosophy behind either of them. Both are against capitalism because of the "selfishness" of capitalists, Tawney preferring the gentlemanly bureaucrat, Veblen the no-nonsense engineer. "What of Davenport's *The Permanent Revolution: Capitalism*?" I ask myself, but am still dissatisfied. He is too sanguine. But there is Kenneth Galbraith's *Countervailing Power*; it could be used to countervail it. Robert Brady's *Organization, Automation and Society,* on the sociology of economics is well worth introducing into this course. So would be chapter II of Max Weber's *Theory of Social and Economic Organization.*

I suppose you would also get in one of the better and more readable books about government regulation of industry and the development of government intervention. Perhaps a case study such as Green and Rosenthal's *Government of the Atom,* would do.

And then you would institute a course in "POLITICAL PSYCHOLOGY", where you would have an even wider range of reading material. You could read to begin with a standard text, like Krech and Crutchfield's on *Social Psychology,* or Ernest Hilgard's *Introductory Psychology,* or something on that order, and then go into books such as Lasswell's on *Power and Personality.* (You thought I was going to say *Psychopathology and Politics* but I didn't; *Power and Personality* might be a little better at this point.) You might read Sebastian de Grazia's *Political Community* or *The Errors of Psychotherapy,* which is an interesting book. Out-of-print it is. However, it will probably be back in print soon. That's a book that he originally called *Government of the Passions,* which was a perfect name because it is a study of authority. It is really directed at the seizure of authority by psychoanalysts and psychiatrists from priests and pastors who seized *their* authority ultimately from medicine men, fakirs, and head shrinkers (of the true type), nor does this long course of development ever get away from the basic fact that it is authority that is being dispensed by these people. Authority is a real medicine; that's the thesis of the book, so he called it *Government of the Passions,* but he went off on a trip to Europe and the Doubleday Company, thinking they might sell more books, renamed it *Errors of Psychotherapy* and that wasn't such a good title. Because the psychologists do not like to admit to errors to the general public, though the limits of therapy are quite obvious to themselves . . . . If it is reprinted as *Government of the Passions,* it becomes more of political science.

In "POLITICAL HISTORIOGRAPHY," which would be another one of our courses, you would use works such as Gottschalk's book on *The Writing of History* or Langlois and Seignobos on the same subject.[3] You might use Gaetano Mosca's *Ruling Class* to get across the idea of how to write general comparative political history, or you might take up some work such as Maude Clarke's *Medieval Representation and Consent* to get a tight study of an important document in the history of representative government, the *Modus Tenendi Parlamentum.* Perhaps Fustal de Coulange's *Ancient City* has value here in uniting history and urban political sociology.

You would move on to a course of study on "LEGAL PROCESS." It is unfortunate that practically all the law that political scientists learn, often all the way through to the doctorate is something about public law, which usually consists of classroom argument over civil liberties problems and a smattering of appellate cases of the Supreme Court. The enormous field of law, by which is meant the subjects of compulsion in society, judicial process, criminology, legal process, the nature of the lawyer as agent, the general sociology of this immense institution, escapes us all until it is too late to recapture. Comparative legal institutions are also slighted, with the exception that sometimes in a course on comparative government you get a certain amount of fact to remember concerning formal structure. You know—what is the *cours de cassation,* and what's the judicial function of the House of Lords, and a few other little scratches on the mind.

But there you would want your students to read something like Edward Levi's *Legal Reasoning* (a University of Chicago type who is also the Provost there now), Roscoe Pound's *Common Law in America,* a lovely little book, or Benjamin Cardozo's *Judicial*

[3] *Introduction* to *The Study of History.*

Process, which is one of the foundations of the activist court of today.

Then you would move on into your senior year, this having been the work of the junior year, and take up there a course on political doctrines. "POLITICAL DOCTRINES" would be your typical course on the history of political philosophy, where you would study Sabine's *History of Political Theories,* which is known to a number of you, I suspect, or a similar work. I won't pause to name others, but would suggest an approach to this course. You should avoid making of the chronological ordering more than it is: it is a convenience; it helps to explain how ideas grow and spread. That is, we shouldn't imply that there is somehow a sort of historical, chronological, date-and-fact-remembering mold that freezes the whole world of philosophy. But, no matter how organized, the course should reveal the great variety of political ideas, and stimulate the political imagination. It should inspire, comfort, insinuate, and correct one's beliefs. In all of this disputation over doctrine, some people are better than others. And some people are real philosophers, as opposed to tract-writers and journalists; one of the reasons for the present abominable taste in judging political writing is the absence of any exposure to great political argumentation of the past. Thus a C. P. Snow essay or Drury's *Advise and Consent* are placed on a par with the *Federalist Papers* or Voltaire's *Candide.* Admittedly, using works that are "hot off the press" helps the uninspired teacher, just as adding more violence and carnage aids the poor script writer on television.

You must beware, though, of the tendency to teach that, in the clash of doctrines throughout history, the better philosophers win out. (I am using "better" in both senses; as more *virtuous* and as more *skilled.*) They usually don't. But political scientists often tell you to forget about all those other bad philosophers despite the fact that they usually won the political struggles. So we have to take the view here that doctrines to the political scientists include both good and bad and are to be judged for their effectiveness in persuading people as well as not. And, further, that doctrines are only one element in the struggle in which everything goes—or as Machiavelli put it, where "unarmed prophets fail, armed prophets prevail." There is a kind of continuity all the way from the grunt type of political doctrine—you know, the blood and soil, *blut und boden* fantasies, through all the propagandistic doctrinal presentations of the type of Tom Paine, the great pamphleteer, to the lofty doctrines of Immanuel Kant, Hegel, Aristotle, or Plato. Political Scientists should know not only what political writing is good philosophy but what is effective propaganda, and *why* in each case.

Then would come a course on the "APPLICATIONS OF POWER." Now here we take up our distinction between applied and pure political science. This course might perhaps use a book such as Machiavelli's *Prince* or Ignazio Silone's *School for Dictators,* or Lasswell's *Politics: Who Gets What, When, and How.* So many books might be used here: lots of how-to-do-it books,—you know, *How to Run a Campaign, How to Win Wars, How to Get Ahead in a Bureaucracy, How to Bribe Public Officials*—this sort of question should be involved in a course on applications. Paul Tillitt has just collected many of the better expressions on the subject of practical politics in a work called *The Political Vocation.*

And the purpose is to tell your students that politics, like any other art of influence, involves knowing how to manipulate symbols, how to handle money and material resources, and how to use coercion. Hopefully less of the last than of the others, because we dislike violence, and hopefully too the manipulation of symbols might one day evolve to the point of the application of logico-empirical methods to human affairs. That's the way politics is usually taught, as "holier-than-thou" rational commentaries; yet this must be only a small part of our course, because this course is talking about politics as you find it and how to win in politics and so on, and the course will undoubtedly end on a peroration in which you are enjoining everyone, for God's sake, to try to add some smidgin of reason to politics, and let that be their gift, their departing gift, to the political scene, but stress that they may not win many political engagements by the over-employment of rational method and reason. Else you will be a liar, which is a poor posture for a teacher, even though your students, thoroughly ideologized, may never find you out, or if they did, would never dream that you *should* have been anything *but* a liar.

Then would come a course on "POLITICAL EPISTEMOLOGY." Here one would toss off works such as Dewey and Bentley's *The Knowing and the Known* and Hans Vaihinger's *Philosophy of 'As If'*, a study of fictional and mythical thought. You could keep your feet on the ground with Berelson and Steiner's large compendium of scientific findings called *Human Behavior*. This is a work of several hundred propositions culled only from empirical studies of the last generation. Ask in each case, what does the study *really* tell us? And the intent of this course on political epistemology is to tell us what it is possible to know, how do we know it, what is a fact, what is political logic, and what are the semantics of political science.

Then would come a course on "TECHNIQUES OF STUDY IN POLITICAL BEHAVIOR." And you can be sure that, by this time, even though the student is only a senior in college, he is already far more sophisticated in handling conceptual and research problems in political science than are most Ph.D's and he would therefore be a good candidate for rather difficult works and you could really give him a course in epistemology and you could give him a course in the techniques of studying political behavior. The reading for such a course could be a series of manuals on working "in the field" —Hyman on interviewing, Jennings on sociometry, Berelson on content analysis, and so forth. Document research would be part of it, and also library research.

Then there would be a course of "CASE STUDIES IN AMERICAN GOVERNMENT." A variety of good case materials exists. For example, Stephen Bailey's study of the Full Employment Act of 1946; *Congress Makes a Law* it's called, and it is clear and excellent, Harold Stein's casebook in administration offers several possibilities. But there are many materials here: intensive studies of a congressional committee, of how the President makes up his mind, or of how lobbies operate, and how agencies fight for their budgets.

This course is not going to regurgitate the descriptive kind of political science that your students have had in their first year of college or in high school. Nothing can turn away promising political scientists more in college than having to read the typical textbook in American Government and to take the first course in American Government not once but twice. This has been generally voted the least popular course on campus wherever anybody has dared to take polls on the subject.

Now we have electives for our students but we don't give them too much rope. We have one elective in the second half of the senior year and this elective course must be on the "PRINCIPLES OF ADMINISTRATION," pure and applied. But we are most generous, so we say that these principles need not be learned solely in reference to public administration and national government, such as actually constitutes the course almost everywhere today. He may take such a course if he wishes, but we are not interested in protecting the size of classes of our colleagues so we tell him that he can take this course in educational administration, he can take it in business administration, he can take it in psychology, industrial relations, church administration, in whatever area he pleases as long as it is a pretty good course in the principles of administration. We would hope that they would get into such books as Dimock and Koenig's text on administration, but even more into Rensis Likert's, George Homans', Peter Blau's, Victor Thompson's and Simon and March's studies.

Then in the latter part of the year we would grant them two elective courses. We tell them that they must take a course on "WESTERN EUROPE." An elective? Yes. *Any* elective, after all, is only within the limits of the college catalog. You've seen the programs of some of these new "Freedom Schools" haven't you?, how to mix Molotov cocktails, how to take LSD, and so forth. So no course in the last analysis is quite elective; ours will be even less elective in one sense, but more so in another because we are not saying that students have to take comparative government, which almost always means the government of France and England with perhaps dribs and drabs on Switzerland or Germany and Italy, depending on the prejudices of the instructor, or something on Russia or Sweden if he is a great cooperator and so on.

No. We say that a student may take an intensive course on *one* government; let that government however be a highly developed government, with a highly developed economy.

And we say that he must take another course but this course may deal with any *poor* country. It can be on India, it can be China, it may be on Indonesia or Ghana, but it must be a poor country. Call it a course on "DYSTOPIA."

So you leave him, happy senior, with a diploma in hand, waving good-bye, and hardly, of course, have we turned our backs on him than he is back to register for his graduate work. (Question from floor:

"Do you have any suggestions about the freshman and sophomore years, any ideas about preparation for the above two years?")

The first two years? If you are all interested, then I could talk about the meaning of liberal education, but not tonight. I have a lot of ideas on that score because I think the term "liberal arts" is a most abused term; it should be dispensed with. There are many, many things to be said about the first two years. However, I would say that in practically every university a student in his third year could fit into this program without much trouble. (Question from floor:

"With all this, would anything be *needed* in the first two years?")

You are being sarcastic. You would be doing *something* in the first two years and a lot of that should be English composition, aesthetics of art and music, a foreign language, or linguistics, an introduction to philosophy, surveys in the biological sciences and physical sciences, and so on: plenty of room for excellent courses. This is what would be called a broad curriculum, by the way, very broad. It should be imparted by occasional lectures, much reading, and some serious discussions, and lots of laboratory work in both the arts and sciences.

Now, we come into our first year of graduate study. Look, our guy hasn't had four courses in international relations, has he? And he's gotten an A.B. In fact, he has had no course in international relations, yet I would bet that he would do better as a graduate student in international relations than most students do. Most courses in political science in college are simply journalistic courses and "talk-fests." You can read the *New York Times* and pass them all with a "B". Now I'm counting on everybody reading the *New York Times* in his spare time, not on class time, and reading popular magazines and engaging in dialectics or soapbox agitation in their spare time. Those are for recreational hours.

Well, what would we offer in the graduate curriculum? In the first year (this would be the year of the master's degree), we would give "LOGIC AND QUANTITATIVE METHOD FOR POLITICAL SCIENTISTS." This is a critical study for one's intellectual development, yet there are all too few persons qualified to teach it. The typical course in mathematics for political scientists (or social scientists) commits at least two basic errors: It gives a frightened and awed glance at what graduate students in physics are studying and heads straight for the most special and abstract kinds of mathematics. It plunges into one or two techniques that are *au courant*—say, factor analysis or FORTRAN computer programming—and leaves behind a shattered group of students and most of the problems of political science.

The course proposed here would begin with the forms of logic used in the solution of problems in political science. The logic would be Aristotelian and non-Aristotelian (Dewey and Korzybski). It would evolve into symbolic logic and half-way through the course would transform itself into mathematics. Thereafter it would branch into a case in political statistics, one in decision-making, and one in content analysis. (Other possible branches exist.) Throughout the course, we should prefer "gut-understanding" to mechanical technique. A book such as Abraham Kaplan's *The Conduct of Inquiry* is much to the point here.

We would at the same time offer a course on "LIBRARIANSHIP AND INFORMATION RETRIEVAL FOR POLITICAL SCIENCE." What do you learn from such a course? Is it a drudgery? Well even if it were a drudge course it might not be such a bad idea because it is surprising how many people can't look up a book in a card catalog. But it is more than that. It is classification theory, it's the problems of defining fields, it's the problems of hunting material, it's the practice of vocabulary translation, it's the introduction to computer technology.

You know how much of your time is devoted to searching titles; the only difference between you and me is that I can pay people to search for titles. So my time isn't spent so much on that, but I still spend a great deal of time on bibliography, finding the right work, to save myself embarrassment, true, but also and mostly to find my way to the point as quickly as possible.

There would be a course on the "LITERATURE OF POLITICAL SCIENCE," to reveal the great variety of books, articles, and documents that are considered to be good political science. So hundreds of books would be thrown at one; there would be an open-shelf arrangement and everyone would be dashing about opening books, seeing how people handle problems in political science, tasting a hundred styles, seeing how the age determines the characteristics of a man's mind and so on. All materials would be available in the joint workshop of the courses in the literature of political science and librarianship and information retrieval. It would be part of that fine physical establishment in political science which no university has yet set up but is long overdue. We need prompt access to our libraries, we need to put a good part of the tuition of the student into making it possible for him to get what he wants—and more than that, to get it quickly! It is absurd that one should spend a fifth of his time in a course looking for relevant books, often not finding them. But let us go on.

"THE SCOPE OF POLITICAL SCIENCE" would be the name of the last course of the first semester of the graduate curriculum. It would describe the history of political science, explain the curriculum, present and analyze critically the psychology, sociology, economics and ethics of the profession, and point out the traits of the several "schools" of political science, trying not to make more of such schools than they are, that is, not much. Charles Merriam's *Systematic Politics* or my own review of the field[4] would be pertinent works. So would Lasswell and Kaplan's *Power and Society*.

Then we would move into the second semester where the first course would be on "IDEOLOGY, POLITICAL DOCTRINES AND POLITICAL FORMULAS." This would be more sophisticated material related to the earlier course on doctrines. Thus one might use Lasswell's *World Politics and Personal Insecurity* and Karl Mannheim's *Ideology and Utopia*. We would read Tawney's *Religion and the Rise of Capitalism,* and Roberto Michel's *Political Parties,* both of which concern themselves with movements of ideas and their material and psychological determinants. This course would, like the others, emphasize studies of original materials. Probably content analysis would be worked into the proceedings, for it is by this technique that the inquiring mind is buttressed on matters of documentary analysis.

Then we should offer a course on "COMPARATIVE POLITICAL-CULTURAL SYSTEMS." Historical and contemporary cultures would be surveyed in developing the meaning of culture, the destruction of various cultures, and the relation between the political aspects of any culture and the rest of the culture. We would give a course on "COMPARATIVE POLITICAL PARTIES AND PUBLIC OPINION," where books by Duverger, Key, Rokkan, Lipset and Cantril apply, and a course on "COMPARATIVE GOVERNMENTAL INSTITUTIONS," where we would come to grips intellectually with the organs of the state—legislative, executive, judicial. In this course we should engage Wheare on *Legislatures,* Riggs on *Administration* and Mills on *Representative Government,* to name a few.

Notice my emphasis upon the comparative method. That's the way to stretch people's minds so as to make them aware of differences, to make them generalize, to make them flexible when it comes to solving problems by themselves. Recent handbooks of comparative statistics of the structure of nations by Banks, Textor,

[4] *Political Behavior* and *Political Organization.*

Russett, Deutsch and others are valuable sources of information, generalization and quantitative testing for this course; the data of these books is now available in punch-card form for student projects, a practice newly initiated but prognostic of the future.

Our student is ready for his Master's Degree, if only we would decide whether to require a thesis of him. I am inclined to favor an option either to present for approval three term-papers from his graduate or senior-year courses (which would permit an excellent honors thesis to qualify), or to write a thesis that displays theory and technique in brief scope.

And while I am about it, I should add an opinion with respect to linguistic qualifications. As you know to your regret, the so-called language requirement in most universities is hidebound by cultural habits of a half-century ago. Foreign languages remain useful tools for many purposes but it should be up to the student and his advisor to determine whether he must know a language other than English, what it should be (it *could* be *any* language or dialect), whether only one is sufficient, or whether, indeed, his interests are such as to require alternative and equivalent practice of a given skill, say, statistics, linguistics and philology in general, computer theory, or a type of field work or apprenticeship. For that matter, considering the stress that our new curriculum lays upon "tools", this kind of *quid pro quo* only remains to symbolize illogically the resolution of the struggle of the new against the traditional approach to political science.

Granted the M.A. degree, our student commences his final year of formal work in a double course, "POLITICAL SOCIETY I." But this is really an elective, because he may take up the politics and government of any community. That is, he may take a course in international politics or international organization. In the associational area he may study the government of welfare associations; he may also study corporation government, the government of schools and colleges, or religious government. He may take up one of the major political cultures of the world, or become an expert on American national government, Mexican government, Chinese government, Russian government and so on. Or he may immerse himself in municipal goverment, or provincial and state government. He may seize upon a historical community or a contemporary one. He would follow that in the second semester with more work of the same kind in the course "POLITICAL SOCIETY II;" preferably he would continue in the same topical area.

Then he would take courses in analysis. He would take "ADVANCED PRINCIPLES OF ORGANIZATIONAL BEHAVIOR AND APPLICATIONS." There he would begin to get into problems such as the human relations movement in administrative management, the dynamics of organizational behavior, group dynamics, how to make reports, and how to do research within organizations.

Yet another requirement would be the study of "CONFLICT AND NEGOTIATION: BEHAVIOR AND APPLICATIONS." Conflict after all is not something that you find only in international affairs. You have it throughout society, in every institution; it's all over the place, and it has positive as well as negative aspects. If you read Nicolson's *Diplomacy,* you might well read the Lippitt group's work on *Planned Change.* There is drawing up of a general theory of conflict and a vast literature on it. The journal *Conflict Resolution* is worth your perusing in these respects. Negotiation includes not only diplomacy, but all other forms of negotiation—arbitration, mediation, collective bargaining, the customs that control disputes, such as political deals for presidential nominations and agency appointments, and so on. There is a negotiating aspect which, like the conflict aspect, is part of all political process.

And then we would have a course on "PARTICIPANT OBSERVATION AND REPORTING." Participant observation and reporting constitute a widely accepted and yet unsystematized and untaught part of the repertoire of the political scientist. He must always be prepared to study an organization from within. He must take part in politics or hold a post in administration, and then be able to extricate himself from it and tell what went on. (I am waiting for a student arrested in a riot to plead that he was throwing a brick as field work in PARTICIPANT OBSERVATION.)

People think they can draw up a questionnaire, that they can somehow go out and draw it up well. I could tell you much about the examinations that I have given in the past, in which I have simply asked people who were supposed to know a body of theory and facts to ask questions about the material. When asked to give back a good set of questions on what they are supposed to have learned, they are nonplussed.

What holds for a questionnaire holds for every part of this process. Interviewing?—well, you just go over to somebody and you ask them, you know, what you wanted to learn, or anything that's on your mind. I was just reading a Ph.D. examination wherein the victim had been asked to design a research project, so he said, "and I would have my students go out and ask questions of these judges to find out whether they are liberal or conservative." Ugh! You can imagine what will happen if they ever get in to see a judge (problems of access are considerable), and they start asking directly "Well judge, just tell me, are you a liberal or are you a conservative?" Reply: "Hm'm. . . . . Where did you say you go to school, boy?" *Reporting* is, of course a very important part of political science. We need to borrow books from journalism for this part of the course: Chilton Bush once wrote a handy one for local government reporters.

Now the remaining courses that I would recommend would include another course on legal processes, called the "ANALYSIS OF LAW AND SANCTIONS." Here we come back in the final semester to what we had something of in undergraduate work; we had the great problems of sanctioning behavior. And remember that power implies sanctions, which is one reason why we are so mixed up mentally most of the time: we are the specialists on authority and sanctions; there isn't anything hotter to handle, they are hotter than fissionable materials. You can stand away from the nuclear furnace, put lead in the way, wear asbestos suits and do a lot of other things, but you can't do so with your political materials. You have got to construct these barriers mostly in your mind, through discipline and study.

And, therefore, the study of law and sanctions, the sanctioning process, what can be gotten out of people by any one of a thousand different modes of persuasion and reward, or punishment and incentive is neglected in political science. When Congress passes a law, it usually throws in whatever sanctions anybody happens to think about at the moment, on what the old law had, or whatever similar laws use. They don't know what the effect of sanctions are. We don't know for example what stops people from taking drugs or alcohol. Most crimes we have no conception of sanctioning. The science of sanction is very young,—guess who wrote a book on the subject? Harold Lasswell, of course. He has a confounding instinct for important subject-matters and, by virtue of being a bachelor of impeccable study-habits and self-discipline, he manages not only to think of a good thesis but to do something about it. So pick up his book on sanctions sometime. Compare it with the classic works of Beccaria, Bentham, and Lombroso.

Then there would be a course on "PEDAGOGY OF POLITICAL SCIENCE." Begin this with a philosophy of the educative process. Use the American pragmatists as your guide; the classical educators cut down the innocent from an austere distance, letting only the agile self-teachers escape, wounded. Ask now "How do you present the materials that you have learned up to this point, how do you advise students to get in or to get out of the field, and what techniques do you use in examining them?" Considering the obsession with grades throughout American education, it is stunning to realize the ignorance of examining technique.

And finally a course in "RESEARCH DESIGN." In this course the student spends his time proposing and drawing up different kinds of projects to solve specified problems. Here you may become as sophisticated as you please. He may go so far as to design a project with a pre-set budget in mind (because we always are dealing with fixed and limited resources) and then applying that project. One could initiate pilot projects whereby the student goes out and tests his questionnaire, tests his design, tests the response, tests his tools of analysis, and comes back and reworks the design and says, "All right, this design is ready to go."

APPENDIX

*Synopsis of Recommended Curriculum for Concentration in Political Science: Junior Year to Doctoral Preliminary Examinations**

Junior Year

1. Power
2. Political Anthropology
3. Political Geography
4. Political Sociology
5. Political Economy
6. Political Psychology
7. Political Historiography
8. Legal Process

Senior Year

1. Political Doctrines
2. Applications of Power
3. Political Epistemology
4. Techniques of Study in Political Behavior
5. Case Studies in American Government
6. Principles of Administration
7. Western European Government "X"
8. Dystopic Government "X"

Master's Year

1. Logical & Quantitative Method for Political Scientists
2. Librarianship & Information Retrieval for Political Scientists
3. Literature of Political Science
4. Scope of Political Science
5. Ideology, Political Doctrines and Political Formulas
6. Comparative Political Systems Cultures
7. Comparative Political Parties and Public Opinion
8. Comparative Governmental Institutions

(Thesis optional)
(Languages tailored to need)

Doctor's Year

1. Political Society I
2. Advanced Principles of Organization: Behavior and Applications
3. Conflict & Negotiations: Behavior and Applications
4. Participant Observation and Reporting
5. Political Society II
6. Legal Analysis and Sanctions
7. Pedagogy of Political Science
8. Research Design

(Dissertation required)

* I am opposed to rigid requirements and the everyday lecture system, hence I would like to see my ideal curriculum installed in our minds rather than instituted as coercive rote.

And if he can do a good study design, a really sophisticated study design, in some ways it is better than a thesis in showing that he is ready for full professional status as a social scientist.

The conclusion of his formal education is then near at hand. The curriculum has taken him up to the point where he is ready to write his dissertation. He should know exactly how to go about it. The factual content of the dissertation should cause him very little trouble because he is so splendidly equipped to find it wherever it may be and whatever form it may be in. He is ready to handle it, to put it into the right shape and form. He will be a veritable Modigliani, artist of a masterpiece between cocktails and supper. And from that point on, you will be Lord of the Flies at Red River U.

II. THE AMERICAN IMAGE PROJECT

"The American Image" is the name assigned to a proposed large-scale study of the American people to be undertaken for educational and scientific purposes.

Goals

The sponsors of the project[5] wish to invite a cross-section of the American people to cooperate with a group of social and behavioral scientists in recording on film, in speech, and through interview their individual parts in the vast and complex republic. With the materials collected from this survey and concurrent studies, the sponsors plan to make available over an indefinite period of time:

1. Scientific reports on the sociological characteristics of the population, especially the socio-economic settings in which people are found, and the group life in which they move.

[5] The original proposal was drafted in 1964; this is a draft of July, 1966. Two substantial spenders of research funds, one a government agency, the second a corporation for educational publishing punctuated enthusiastic readings with clutches at their purse. The author wishes to thank Harold D. Lasswell and Angus Campbell who agreed to co-sponsor the proposal and whose enlightening friendship extends beyond this case and over many years.

2. Anthropological studies of the physical character of the population, speech habits, dress, and ways of comportment.
3. Economic studies of the occupations, spending habits, and uses to which goods are put.
4. Humanistic studies of the aesthetics of the American, his tastes, his uses of cultural materials.
5. Civic studies on the political awareness, activity and attitudes of the people.

And in conjunction with these scientific studies, several forms of applied work, that is,

6. Relation of all the foregoing to educational achievements and suggestions for curricula.
7. Dynamuseums, that is, scientifically prepared social displays, which can be made mobile and used in schools of the land to show who the Americans are, how they live, think, and work.
8. Displays, including giant schoolroom wall charts that show a cross-section of the American people, to answer the eternal question addressed to the teacher: What is an American?"
9. A series of reports based on these and associated materials, published for both school teachers and the elementary and secondary school student in works of graded difficulty of comprehension.
10. State and regional seminars for the exposition of the results of the studies to school officials and teachers.
11. To build up and maintain a permanent Dynamuseum of Man in New York as a center in itself and as a clearinghouse for all the local American and international services to be provided by the project.

Means

The means by which the sponsors plan to achieve such results are as follows, subject to further planning and decisions:

1. The establishment of an educational corporation independent of existing institutions, with a Board of Trustees composed of distinguished scientific leaders, centered in New York.
2. Financing of the program through the United States Office of Education, the National Science Foundation, other government

agencies, and various non-government foundations, all of whom share the research and education objectives of the sponsors.

3. Co-opting a complete executive committee and appointing a director and subordinate officials.
4. Instituting a set of directives for achieving the program and budgeting the phases of the operations.
5. Contracting with the Survey Group "X" for undertaking the national sample survey. Contracting with educational film group "Y" to provide training, crews, and production for the film work to be completed in the survey. Contracting with information storage, retrieval and publishing group "Z" for the preparation of reports and materials for publication. Contracting with Group "Q" for the administration of the project (housekeeping, accounting, purchasing, etc.).
6. Organizing a central scientific and professional staff which, because of the above contracting arrangements, will be able to give undiluted attention to the theory, goals and substantive execution of the program.
7. Carrying out the phases of the program as outlined below.

Phases

The phases of *The American Image Project* are planned as follows, subject to further determination:

Phase 1. Six Months: Planning and designing the proposal in detail, and presenting it to interested agencies for discussion, approval, and support. During this phase, the Board of Trustees will be settled upon.

Phase 2. Three months: Financing, incorporation, and organizing phase. Offices opened.

Phase 3. Five months:

A. Contracting for administration, survey, publication, and film production.

B. Organizing and conducting a training school for the employment of motion pictures in social surveys. Crews would be selected and trained here for the actual work of the project.

Phase 4. Four months: Pilot studies.

Phase 5. Six months: Field work. In this critical phase, the bulk of material for the whole project would be gathered in a national film and questionnaire personal interview of a sample of Americans.

Phase 6. One year: Analysis of materials by a battery of new techniques employing the computer and other instruments. Preparation of reports of scientific findings. Preparation of educational displays, and other educational materials.

Phase 7. One Year: Publication of scientific reports. Publication and display of materials. Planning of new projects.

Total time elapsed from date of this memorandum: Four years.

Costs

Estimated costs of *The American Image Project*: (to be recalculated precisely in Phase 1.)

Phase 1. Original planning and designing: Consulting time, travel, secretarial, other; $7,000, absorbed by sponsors and interested agencies.

Phase 2. Financing, incorporating, organizing: Consultants, legal fees, leases, travel, communications, reports, conferences, office equipment; $29,000, to be paid by interested support agencies.

Phase 3. Administration, planning, contracting, training school:

A. Contracting	$ 8,000
B. Initial payment to contractors	60,000
C. Central Staff	50,000
D. Administrative contractor	20,000
E. Training School (100 students, subsistence, travel to school, faculty, administration, equipment, one month)	120,000
Total cost of Phase 3	$258,000

Phase 4. Pilot Studies:

A. Central Staff	$ 70,000
B. Survey contractor	40,000
C. Film contractor	20,000
D. Administrative contractor	20,000
Total cost of Phase 4	$150,000

Phase 5. Field Work:

A. Central Staff	$ 80,000
B. Survey contractor	100,000
C. Film contractor	400,000
D. Administrative contractor	40,000
E. Reports and publications contractor	20,000
Total cost of Phase 5	$640,000

Phase 6. Analysis and preparation of reports and materials:

A. Central Staff	$200,000
B. Survey contractor	100,000
C. Film contractor	250,000
D. Administrative contractor	80,000
E. Reports, Publications and Displays contractor	175,000
Total cost of Phase 6	$805,000

Phase 7. Publications, Storage, and Display:

A. Central Staff	$400,000
B. Survey contractor	100,000
C. Film contractor	100,000
D. Administrative contractor	60,000
E. Reports, Publications and Display contractor	225,000
Total cost of Phase 7	$885,000

Total cost of *The American Image Project* over four years:

$2,738,000

Principles

In embarking upon a project of such extent, the sponsors are convinced of the importance of a number of propositions concerning American society, the principles of social science, and the needs of American education. These propositions underlie the far-flung operations that are contemplated and justify the heavy investment of national talents and funds. They are stated as follows:

1. The social crisis in America today calls urgently for a recreation of an "American Image" based upon the realities and aspirations of Americans as they are.
2. Never before has a true census in depth of the American people in their full variety and life settings been accomplished. Statistics of the census type and survey data in most instances skim the surface of the truths about the people.
3. Many Americans suffer from stereotypes about their fellow citizens, most of which beliefs are harmful to social solidarity and block freedom of opportunity and equal dignity for all.
4. Many Americans hold mistaken beliefs about themselves and their place in the country, suffering from low estimates of themselves, and resulting feelings of inferiority and insecurity.
5. A full and sympathetic vision of oneself and others as parts of the communities of the land will constitute and can be used to aid in a form of mental health therapy, especially in problems of schizophrenia, alienation, aggressiveness, and related areas.
6. The "Hollywood Image" of the American people has done harm to the people in many cases and there has been until now no image *in kind* to contradict it. By the same token, some measure of control over the "Madison Avenue image" can be sought in a presentation of Americans as they are.
7. Because of the crude, thoughtless, and haphazard spreading of American characterizations around the world, foreign nations and peoples misjudge Americans badly. They receive

defective, unsympathetic, and inhuman portraits of Americans. A thesaurus of scientific, graphic, and written material characterizing the American way of life can be helpful to American foreign policy and American cooperation with other peoples of the world.

8. The American people are in a state of great mobility. The "melting pot" is working not only ethnically, but religiously, occupationally, geographically, and culturally. A complete and detailed "shot" of the nation at this point will be of inestimable value to the reassessment, future planning, and social history of the country.
9. Planning and policy are more and more being handled by decision-makers who must be divorced from daily contact with the people. The decision-makers need a constant source of graphic refreshment in the subjects of the policies. Students everywhere need to ask themselves constantly whether the academic principles that they are about to apply correspond to the people moving before them.
10. The humanities that interest themselves in the language and behavior of the population of different sections of the country need "base lines" by which to evaluate literature and must depend upon sporadic reporting of these features at present.
11. The science of anthropology lacks several basic sources for its development of an anthropology of modern America. It needs accurate and representative data on the physiognomy, posture, gestures, facial expressions, manner of speech, linguistic usages, and dress of Americans.
12. Sociology has been balked in its progress towards an accurate and fundamental set of propositions about American life because it has had to rely on incomplete verbal or second-hand descriptive data on the socio-economic and group settings in which Americans live. Intensive and prolonged analysis of a full data bank, including graphic and accoustical material, will permit large forward steps.
13. The study of representative government, representation, leadership and other political and civic phenomena can

benefit from the matching of appearances, gestures, language, behavior of persons seeking or holding public office and the corresponding handling of expression, symbols, and speech by the represented population.

14. Teachers in the very earliest grades, where the pupils are most impressionable, are often young, inexperienced, and poorly educated themselves, yet must answer complicated social questions such as "What are Americans?" The stereotyped, biased, and partial answers that ensue often do as much harm as good.
15. The inadequacy of library and graphic material sources on social sciences and human relations in the lower schools is notorious, but there is little to supply.
16. Training in the visual arts, the making of surveys by film, is almost completely *terra incognita,* even after motion pictures and still photography have become billion-dollar industries of world-wide importance.
17. Progress has been made in the use of film for scientific and educational purposes in the natural sciences, owing in large part to governmental support, whereas the social sciences have remained unsupported and stagnant in this respect.
18. The methodology of film (both still and motion picture) is badly underdeveloped in the social sciences. It would be a new and valuable manpower resource to have a hundred and more professional social scientists training in the direct employment of and analysis of motion picture and still photography technique for conducting field studies and teaching in the social sciences.
19. The camera provides a new depth and variety of data for social analysis in many disciplines and subject-areas, but its potential is unfathomed. Part of a large-scale project to develop a cross-sectional filming of Americans should be the preparation of an automated index of existing social film resources for quick retrieval and comparative study.
20. The sample survey, perhaps the most versatile and usable instrument of social research, should reach new heights with the incorporation of filming techniques.

21. Not only sample surveys, but projective methods, small group dynamics, case studies, and other methods-areas of the social sciences can be improved and enlarged in scope through adding the pictorial and accoustical dimensions. Experimental design, content analysis, purposive sampling, interviewing, questionnaire construction, research training, and a number of other technical fields will be advanced.
22. All of the social and historical sciences, in interdisciplinary league, can develop and profit from the study of the American Image. In all of them, for example, speech intonation, facial expression, and other accompaniments of discourse, including the settings of discourse, have been accessible only indirectly through the medium of print until now, whereas it is possible to proceed directly from the act itself into the analysis by employing new techniques thoroughly.
23. New techniques of motion picture production are needed. The naive realistic film with the detached commentary is only one of many ways in which to produce communication via film, especially with sound tracks. Many new techniques and principles of sight and accoustics are known today that have not been applied for scientific or educational purposes along the lines of the American Image Project.
24. The traditional natural history and art museums have not been able to engage the social sciences. There is a new species of museum—the Dynamuseum—that can be developed as a teaching device in all grades of study, from elementary to postgraduate education. The concept of a Dynamuseum is needed to teach rapidly and with a great impact. The Dynamuseum concept is the presentation in *tableau pseudovivant* form of a social setting or event, incorporating all of the suggestibility of the "shot" moment of action, with the impact of sound, verisimilitude, smell and accompanying explanation.
25. An institution is needed in which new educational materials can be explained to visiting individual teachers, seminars, and classes. This will include, among other materials, the Dynamuseum.

26. Mobile Dynamuseums and other graphic material can be transported for exhibition purposes around the country bringing the social studies directly to the students.
27. Computer technology has developed to the point where it can be of considerable use in research into American society. Most of the information gathered in such studies can be stored, analysed and retrieved as the demand occurs. Computers can be useful in the analysis of visual appearances, sounds, movements, language, and contents of interviews.
28. Means need to be developed to translate, frame, and produce scientific facts and concepts in the social studies directly into popularly usable form. This translation does not normally occur, partly because of the over-professionalism of the professional and the under-professionalism of the popularizer. If, prior to the initiation of the process of educational production, the final goal is known, the chances of achieving the final goal through rational direction of the processes are greatly increased.
29. Elementary and secondary schools need new curricular materials for civics, American history, economics, psychology, and social studies. These can be provided by new types of materials, phonograph records, tapes, slides, motion picture films, wall displays, pamphlets, books and mobile exhibits.
30. A series of experimental primers for elementary school social studies and for secondary school social sciences can be of great use. The social sciences can be taught together in the early years of education without too great loss of sharpness and validity if they are presented in a proper form with the proper professional controls.
31. It is important at this stage in the development of the behavioral sciences to build up bodies of data of massive extent. The tools of analysis have outmatched the materials for analysis. In effect, giant steam shovels are being used to turn over handfuls of dirt. There is no rich collection of broad, validated, standardized, usable, first-hand facts about American civilization.

END OF PROPOSAL

The Reactants Models

STUART C. DODD
University of Washington

and

STEFAN C. CHRISTOPHER
Seattle University

FOREWORD

This hitherto unpublished article is included in this memorial volume as an illustration of fruitage from the seeds Lundberg planted. It summarizes the largest research inquiry—Project Revere—which Lundberg and Dodd executed in the post-war decades. However imperfectly, it illustrates the application of scientific methods of inquiry by means of increasingly rigorous measurement and controlled experiments that test hypotheses towards discovering laws of human social behavior.

The development of such laws is illustrated here in the behavioral subfield of mass communications. The eight "powers models" [A[a]] that emerged from Project Revere, represent an attempt to so describe in equations the diffusing of an item through a population as increasingly to explain, predict, and control such communicative behavior. These elementary equations of interaction among sets of actors illustrate Lundberg's lifelong quest for highly invariant generalizations, stating in "If, then" form, how specified and operationally observed behaviors will recur under their recurring conditions. Thus the logistic law states: "If actors interact in pairs, communicating an item with equal opportunity and frequency per period, then that item will diffuse through that set of actors and periods as described by the cumulative logistic formula $p_t = 1/(1+q_o/p_o e^{-at})$, as explained by its randomly most probable increments per period, $\triangle_t = kp_tq_t$; and as predicted by its S-shaped growth curve. Insofar as its specified conditions occur, fully and solely, in just so far this "If, then" generalization will hold in any science, whether the sets of actors be molecules, mice, or men.

Lundberg advocated, and through his partner, Dodd, helped to execute, experiments developing such scientific laws of social behavior. When the Behavioral Research Council was formed, he proposed that its early publications include this long-delayed report from Project Revere. It has been delayed for some fifteen years while seeking (after lapsed funding): (a) more definitive experiments; (b) more rigorous mathematical formulation (in terms of stochastic processes and modern probability and systems theory), and (c) richer practical applications. Though still needing much more of these three lines of research, this Memorial volume seems an opportunity to communicate some of these illustrative achievements to date, however unfinished, for others to build upon and refine.

FORECASTING SOME PROBABLE ACTS OF MEN

This paper sets forth a brief summary of Project Revere and an interpretation of some of its findings. The project was done under a grant from the United States Air Force. The Air Force wished to learn the probable effects of propaganda leaflets dropped from planes on people. Among the techniques used were wide dropping of leaflets on some thirty towns in the United States, and the use of polling techniques and mail-back returns to find out their effects.

The Washington Public Opinion Laboratory at the University

of Washington in Seattle conducted extensive experiments over a period of three years (1950-53) of pretesting and testing followed by more than a decade of retesting the chief findings reported here. Although Project Revere had a specific task, its findings are broad enough so as to have wide implications in the form of candidate laws for communication theory in particular, and for the behavioral sciences in general.

I.

The Task

The task assigned by the Air Force to Project Revere was to develop systems of rules called "models" for maximizing the diffusing of messages from airborne leaflets through a target population. These diffusion models were to be judged by six practical criteria, which proved to be highly achievable, namely: How (1) *general,* (2) *prevalent,* and (3) *operational* are these models? The models, of course, should also satisfy well the three methodological criteria of any model that it proves (4) to be *reliable* on reobserving its indices, (5) *valid* when correlated against specified criteria, and (6) *predictive* of outcomes under recurring conditions. The models were designed to answer the following questions: How fast and far, how fully and faultlessly will messages spread through a target population under a set of specified and repeatable conditions? This paper answers only the first question in reporting on models which try to describe so as to explain and predict the speed of spreading, or the temporal course of diffusing.

II.

Findings of Project Revere

This paper orders the chief findings from fitting curves to diffusion data, as reported by Project Revere.[1] From this research, a

[1] Fuller reporting is contained in (see Ref. 20 for listings): Over 60 journal articles involving Project Revere; 27 reports to the Air Force; six Ph.D. and M.A. theses; "Revere Studies on Interaction" a 1,000-page unpublished (dittoed) volume by S. C. Dodd, E. D. Rainboth and J. Nehnevajsa; deposited in the University of Washington Library.

"powers model" or family of eight types of curves were found to fit the data closely. In what follows, these eight submodels will be described. These eight were winnowed from forty series of tests in some thirty communities involving half a million citizens reacting to some half million leaflets. Each curve states a "law of process" in an algebraic formula. Each is sketched in a setting where it was clearly observed. These curves can be thought of as depicting some simple and regular tones and overtones in the reverberating of a message through a community sounding board.

A. *Logistic curves*—an observed regularity of man-to-man or social diffusing—*in groups,* (e.g., one item spreading through conversational pairs).

Over twenty sets of data (Refs. 8, 9), cumulatively plotting increments in time of man-to-man diffusion whether in captive groups or in open communities, tended to show S-shaped curves. Thus one such experiment (Ref. 20), a retest graphed in Figure 1, observed 78 persons, alike in age, sex, non-acquaintance and each of 49 other variables relevant to diffusion in a large furniture-free room, pairing off at will (i.e., "with equal opportunity") in each of eight minute-long periods. The eight observed increments of diffusion agreed closely and significantly with the logistic hypothesis for dyadic groups. The validity correlation between the expected and observed *increments* in knowers here exceeded .996, and was statistically significant at the 1 percent level. The logistic model says roughly: If anyone tells an item to anyone with like-chance and like-speed, then that item will spread as predicted by the S-shaped logistic curve (defined by $\triangle = kpq$—see Fig. 1c).

Summary: These four graphs visualize, in sets of people and periods, the close, ($r^2 > .9$) and significant (5% level) fits of hypothesis and observed data–of model and the measured acts of men in these diffusing or communicational situations.

FIGURE 1

The Positive Powers or Moments Clan, $[\overline{A^{+a}}]$, *of Reactants Submodels showing fits to data of mass communication processes under specified conditions of structuring ratios (items told/items heard) and steady, equal opportunities to act*

The *Normal* Submodel, $\overline{A^{\circ}}^{t}$

(to forecast hearers from n joint tellings)

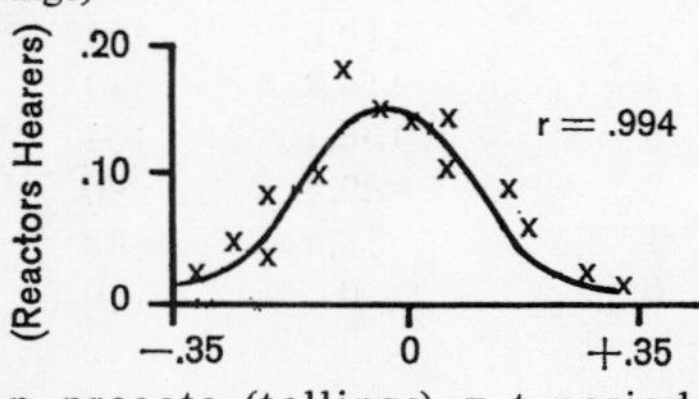

n preacts (tellings) = t periods

$\Delta_{lg} = k(p_1+q_1)$ and $p_t = k\ e^{-t^2/2}$

The *Waning Exponential* Submodel, $\overline{A^{1}}^{t}$

(to forecast hearers from 1 repetitive telling)

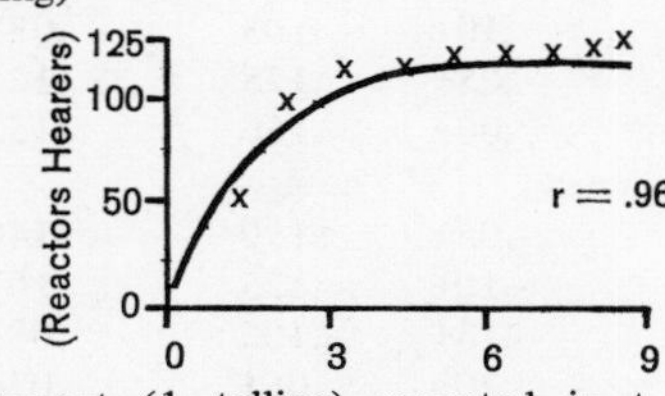

1 preact (1 telling) repeated in t periods

$\Delta_{lg} = kq_1$ and $q_t = k\ e^{-t}$

The *Logistic* Submodel, $\overline{A^{2}}(t)$

(to forecast hearers from paired-off tellers)

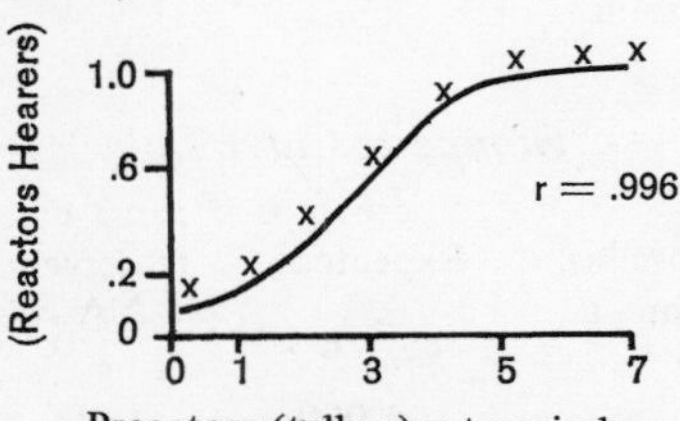

Preactors (tellers) = t periods

$\Delta_{lg} = kp_t q_t$ and $p_t/q_t = p_o/q_o\ e^{kt}$

The *Gompertz* Submodel, $\overline{A^{2}}^{t}$

(to forecast hearers from fully paired-off tellers)

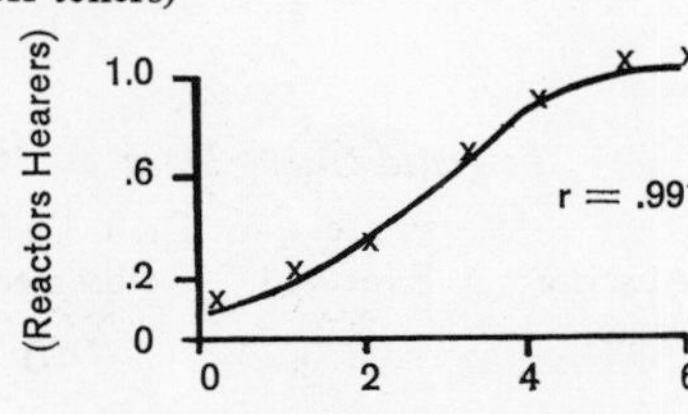

Preactors (tellers) = t periods

$\Delta_{lg} = k\ q_t$ and $q_t = k\ q_1^{2^t}$

Key: Solid line shows the curve expected by the hypothesis; x's show observed data in Project Revere.

A = all-or-none item-act (=1,0); $_1A$ = stimulus preacts (tellings of items); $_2A$ = response reacts (hearings of items); t = times.

Δ_{lg} = a log increment = a factor; p = proportion of actors, knowers; q = 1-p, non-knowers.

k = the "potency constant," a social force of 1 act per actor per period per period.

r = intraclass correlation of increments as hypothesized vs. as observed.

DATA FOR FIGURE 1

Normal Curve Data

Abscissa (size of r)	Frequencies Expected Δ_h	Frequencies Observed Δ_o
.30+	.010	.007
.25+	.016	.015
.20+	.035	.044
.15+	.061	.074
.10+	.103	.088
.05+	.125	.125
.00+	.150	.132
Mean		
-.05+	.150	.140
-.10+	.125	.162
-.15+	.103	.088
-.20+	.061	.074
-.25+	.035	.022
-.30+	.020	.022
-.35+	.010	.007

From W. R. Catton's Ph.D. thesis, p. 131, Fig. 10a/N = 136, r_{ic} = .994 (of increments, Δ).

Exponential Curve Data

Abscissa time, t	Frequencies Expected $\Sigma\Delta_h$	Frequencies Observed $\Sigma\Delta_o$
9	124.6	125
8	124.2	122
7	123.5	122
6	122.2	122
5	119.6	121
4	114.9	117
3	106.1	107
2	89.5	90
1	58.4	48
0	0	0

Fig. 5, Revere sheet. N = 125, r = .96 (of increments, Δ), $r_{\Sigma\Sigma}$ = .995 (of cumulated variables)

Logistic Curve Data

Abscissa time, t	Frequencies Expected $\Sigma\Delta_h$	Frequencies Observed $\Sigma\Delta_o$
7	1.000	1.000
6	1.000	.998
5	.970	.960
4	.826	.811
3	.583	.580
2	.354	.359
1	.196	.203
0	.103	.103

r_{ic} = .9960 (of increments, Δ)
N = 78 freshman girls (Ref. 23).

Gompertz Curve Data

Abscissa time, t	Frequencies Expected $\Sigma\Delta_h$	Frequencies Observed $\Sigma\Delta_o$
6	1.000	1.000
5	.965	.960
4	.813	.846
3	.570	.597
2	.344	.346
1	.190	.189
0	.100	.100

r_{ic} = .9912 (of increments, Δ)
Gompertz, N = 70 freshman, both sexes (Ref. 23).

B. *Exponential curves*—an observed regularity of mass diffusing—in plurels[2] (e.g., one item repeated to many people as in broadcasting an advertisement).

A message diffuses from airborne leaflets either by social diffusion from "passed-on" messages heard (the logistic case above) or by physical diffusion of "picked-up" leaflets read. This physical diffusion was expected to follow the waning exponential curve, as the remaining nonknowers dwindled randomly. This hypothesis expects: "If a random sampling of constant size is repeatedly told an item, then knowledge of it will spread in a waning exponential curve defined by its finite increment of knowers as $\triangle = kq$." (see Fig. 1B) Towards testing this exponential model for predicting increments of diffusion, a correlation of $r = .96$ ($N = 125$) between it and physical diffusion was observed in one town even though the two masking variables of (1) leaflets dwindling on the ground (due to children collecting them, winds, etc.), and (2) social diffusion, were uncontrolled. Thus the exponential model for plurels ($\triangle = kq$,—see Fig. 1B) seems to fit better the more its specified pre-conditions are fulfilled, but the cleaner "unmasking" tests need still to be conducted.

C. *Normal curves*—an observed regularity of multiple diffusing—in *persons* (e.g., many items equally learned by many persons as in school classes).

The normal probability submodel in the field of communication here expects: "If people have equal opportunity to hear or not hear each of many equally weighted items, then the distribution of items heard at any time will approach normality."

This familiar and democratic distribution occurs, for example, when n pennies are tossed N times, or when n items of news or knowledge, of culture or behavior, are communicated with like-chance among N people. This normal distribution can grow up in many ways—as proved by the Central Limit theorem. One simple way is to expand the binomial $(p + q)^n = 1^n = 1$ which can

[2]A plural designates any plural number of humans of one sort without connoting any further characteristics.

represent the unified interaction or product of η all-or-none items (each a mean among N persons—i.e., $(p + q)^1 = 1$ item averaged). A simple formula for the additive increments, $\triangle$, in the normal curve is $\triangle = xp$ the current product of a deviation $x +$ its frequency, p.

A highly structured example, not designed as a test, but illustrating the principle of a normality submodel in Project Revere, was a study of value systems having to do with multiplex preferences in diffusing leaflet messages (see Fig. 1). Three sets of judges rated their preferences for each of seventeen "universal" sorts of appeals, in leaflets with a "Donate to the blood bank" message. The 136 intercorrelation indices $((17^2 - 17)/2 = 136)$ among the appeals were normally distributed. The preference ratings can be interpreted roughly as of "multiplex" origin i.e., as due to many, small, independent influences that are usually called "chance."

D. *Simplex* (*i.e., Gompertz*) *curves*—an observed regularity of full social diffusing—in *organizations* (as among officials and citizens).

A common growth function in biology is the simplex or Gompertz S-shaped curve. It is produced if every doer in a set meets another doer, and, *with the same chance* for all in time span after span, passes on an all-or-none item, whether a state, a thing, or a message. This simplex submodel for communication of "bits" of information (or items of knowledge here) from Project Revere was retested in its simplest form where it closely approximates the full logistic curve with $k = 1$. It was retested in strictly controlled experiments on people (Refs. 22, 25) because of its potential importance i.e., to pair off and pass on an item. It states a universal law of spreading any all-or-none item whether a right, a trait, news or knowledge, or other item whatever through a set of n actors whether human or nonhuman. Its growth rule is $dq/dt = -p \lg p$. This means that its "chance cause" or generating is by (a) many, (b) similar, (c) independent actors, (d) meeting together in all possible pairs. This simplex law might be an answer in many fields of science to questions like: How does a set of n elements grow by random interacting within itself? The generality of these chance-like bits of growth is shown in turn by their many names as bits of information or of "knowledge" or of decision; or bits of "uncertainty" as to that which is not yet known, of pure "complexity," of pure "order," of either "positive or negative entropy," and so forth (Ref. 22).

Thus one set of controlled tests in spreading a message both confirmed the purely chance causation of the Gompertz curve and further measured the effects of its three most common masking causes or overlaying variables, singly and together. Tests in which these three masking causes at first changed jointly and uncontrolled (Refs. 20, 22, 26) showed that the variance of the growth increments (in percents of the population diffused) was accounted for as follows:

1. By chance, i.e., random pairing off or by forming its self product or square t times (as defined by the Gompertz curve), $y = n2^t$	92%
2. By intersex attractions among 70 college students	1%
3. By acquaintance among these 70 college students	1%
4. By sampling fluctuations among these 70 college students	6%
	100%

Further tests almost eliminated these three masking causes by reobserving the whole Gompertz growth curve: (a) in each sex alone, (b) among strangers to each other, (c) with 70 replications of the whole curve each a mean of 70 observed cases or meetings of a pair of persons to make the sampling errorless. As a result, 99.6 percent of the diffusion's variance was accounted for by the estimated Gompertz building up by random pairing off with only four-tenths of one percent left over as due to all errors of sampling, plus errors of observation, plus errors of any other sort whatever.

E. *Harmonic logistic curves*—an observed regularity of resisted, social diffusion—in waning pair groups (as when other interests intervene with time).

The harmonic logistic is a compound submodel (Ref. 15) compounded as a syntactic product showing a behavioral joint occurrence of its two factors, the logistic interacting in pairs and the harmonic increase of some resistance. The harmonic logistic curve, or family of S-shaped and also decelerating growth curves, describes and predicts diffusion in person-to-person groups, or pairs, that goes on at a rate that is in part inverse to the time since it started. The harmonic logistic hypothesis says this as:

> "If everyone tells an item to anyone with equal opportunity in the face of steadily growing resistance, then the item will spread through that set of people in a harmonic logistic curve of slowed-up social diffusion."

F. Positive powers clan- ($\triangle = A^{+a}$) of reactants curves (generalizing submodels A-E above).

A situation showing all the above curves simultaneously is a classroom where every child is expected to have an equal opportunity to learn. The last term of each binomial expansion, shown in the next to the last column in Table 1, measures the proportion of students who still know no facts on the tth day as predicted by the waning exponential curve or submodel. If instead of teacher-student interaction, Table 1 shows student-student communicating of one item, then the last column of q terms measures this social diffusion as foretold by the full logistic curve and also (at bits-log intervals) by the Gompertz curve.[3]

G. *Linear Curves*—an observed order in proportional diffusing.

The most general, common, and operational curve in Project Revere was the linear model. More substantively, a "chain tags" experiment (Ref. 14) used the linear model to observe and measure, to predict and control message-spread in four towns. This linear diffusion submodel states: "If steady tellings have just k first hearings in each unit period, then items known grow linear-

[3] Table 1 can include, we hypothesize, the 3rd and 4th moments' submodels by treating p, the knowings or knowers, as —p to show either disbelief in the message or else hostility to its tellers.

TABLE I

The Positive Powers Clan, $[A^{+a}]$, of Reactant Submodels defining four laws of communication, or interaction generally

t days ↓	t^{th} power of zeroth moment	The binomial expansion, $\overline{A}^{ot} \equiv (p+q)^t$	Its last term (% of facts unheard to date)	Initial last term successively squared, t' (q= proportion of non-knowers of the item)
1	$\overline{A}^{o1}$ =	p_1 +	q_1^1	$q_1^{2^o}$
2	$\overline{A}^{o2}$ =	$p_1^2 + 2p_1q_1$ +	q_1^2	$q_1^{2^1}$
3	$\overline{A}^{o3}$ =	$p_1^3 + 3p_1^2 + 3p_1q_1^2$ +	q_1^3	---
4	$\overline{A}^{o4}$ =	$p_1^4 + 4p_1^3q_1 + 6p_1^2q_1^2 + 4p_1q_1^3$ +	q_1^4	$q_1^{2^2}$
5	$\overline{A}^{o5}$ =	$p_1^5 + 5p_1^4q_1 + 10p_1^3q_1^2 + 5p_1^1q_1^4$ +	q_1^5	---
t	$\overline{A}^{ot}$ =	$p^t + t^o p^{t-1} q^1$ + the other binomial terms +	${q_1}^t$	$q_1^{2^{t'}}$
			↑	↑
large t	$\overline{A}^{ot \text{ (large)}}$ =	The normal submodel in this row predicts a normal distribution of reactions.	The exponential growth curve predicting reacts	The full logistic and Gompertz curves predicting reactors

Showing how random reiterative interacting of a set of elements forms self-products or behavioral stochastic processes which can be measured, produced and predicted as normal, exponential, logistic, Gompertz and other distribution and growth curves or laws by means of the successive positive powers of the set of acts of elemental diffusing called "tell-hears."

---

ly" (k, the potency parameter, measured as new hearers per teller and period, was set up to be exactly unity in each tagged chain). With this tight experimental control of the diffusing, by using "chain-tagged leaflets" the correlation of observed increments in the hearings with expected increments within each chain was necessarily unity, i.e., $r = 1.0$.

H. *Logarithmic curves*—an observed order in "diminishing returns" diffusion.

The project's outline hypothesized that the Weber-Fechner principle of a logarithmic relation of stimulus to response in persons would apply to whole communities. A simple restatement is:

"To add knowers, multiply leaflets."

For one possible reason or causal mechanism, note that natural logarithms are about the same as the sum of the inverse natural numbers t, or harmonic series $1/t$. This means that any steady process that is observed as increments relative to the total to date, yielding the inverse natural numbers, will, if they are then summed, yield the logarithm of the number of periods up to date.

Thus a log relation of stimulation to response, or a diminishing returns law, may be expected whenever, for any steady stimulation over time, the response is observed as the cumulated relative response to the total stimulation up to date.

In an experiment to test this logarithmic hypothesis, planes dropped leaflets, doubling in number per capita, on each of eight matched towns. (Refs. 8, 11, 18, 20) A poll of every second household showed that the percent of knowers increased in equal percentage increments as the leaflets per capita doubled. To add each 9 percent of respondents here required multiplying the leaflet stimulation by two. The log model here fitted the observed data well, the value of r being .97.

I. *Harmonic curves*—an observed order in resisted diffusion.

It was hypothesized on the basis of former studies that any constant output of effort must show a harmonically decreasing effectiveness when a resistive factor grows steadily within it. The rule is: Effective action varies with effort and inversely with resistance. The hypothesis may be stated as:

"If a population's constant effort to tell a message meets steadily increasing counter-acting, other things being equal, then its effective reacting will wane inversely with the counter-active index."

As hypothesized, the effective reacting did wane harmonically with the counteracting. A correlation coefficient of .99 was observed, and the appropriate chi square test shows significance at the five percent level. (Ref. 18)

FIGURE 2

The Negative Powers Clan, $[A^{-a}]$, *of Reactants Submodels showing fits to data of mass communication processes under specified conditions of structuring ratios (i.e., items told/items heard) and steady, equal opportunities to act*

The *Linear* Submodel, $[A^{-0}]$ (to forecast hearings from tellings)

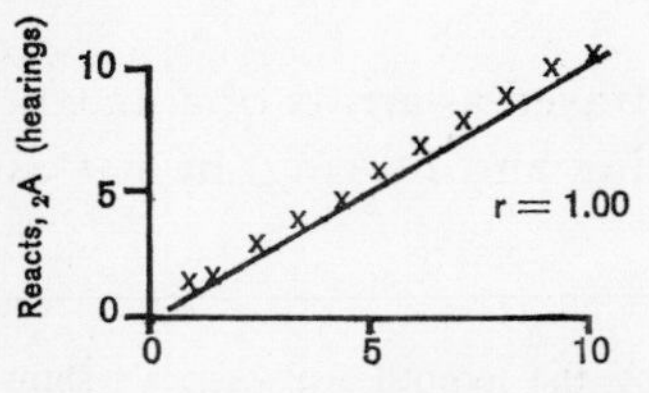

$_1A$=n preacts (tellings) = t periods

$\Sigma\Delta = k$ $\qquad {}_2A \doteq_{\circ} kt$

The *Logarithmic* Submodel, $[A^{-1}]$ (to forecast hearings from cumulated relative tellings)

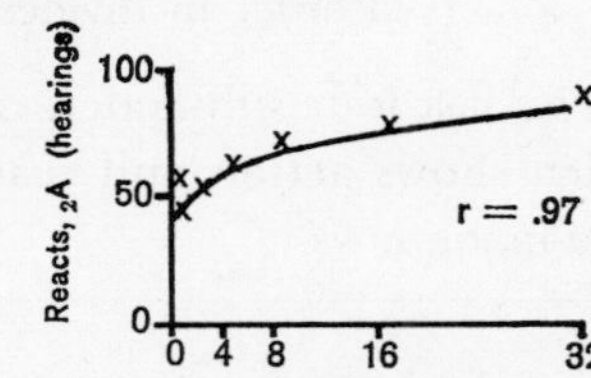

$_1A$=n preacts (tellings) = t periods

$\Sigma\Delta = k/t$ $\qquad {}_2A \doteq_{\circ} k \log t$

The *Harmonic* Submodel, $[A^{-2}]$ (to forecast hearings relative to tellings)

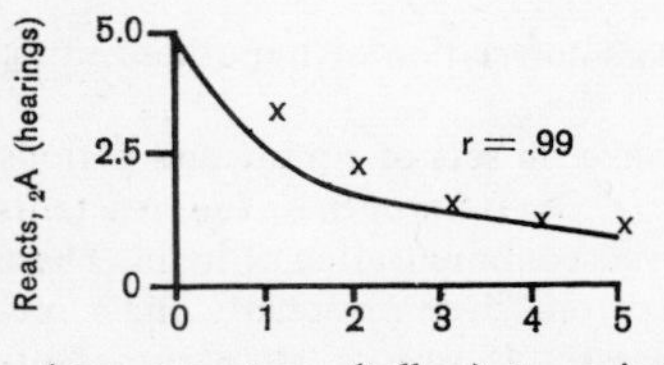

$_1A$=n preactors (tellers)=t periods

$\Delta = k/t^2$ $\qquad {}_2A \doteq_{\circ} k/t$

The *Squared Harmonic* Submodel, $[A^{-3}]$ (to forecast hearings relative to tellers and tellings)

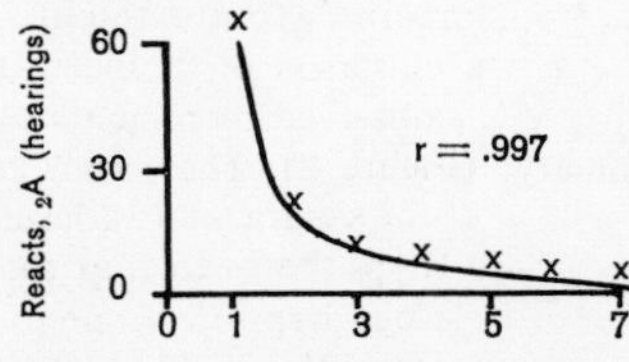

$_1A$=n preactors (tellers) (= t units of distance)

$\Delta = k/t^3$ $\qquad {}_2A \doteq_{\circ} k/t^2$

J. *Squared harmonic curves*—an observed order in doubly waning diffusing.

This squared harmonic model is the harmonic model when the countering action is weighted more heavily as by doubling its exponent (or as a generalized variant, letting its exponent differ from unity to any extent). The general harmonic hypothesis is:

"If people's steady effort to communicate meets steadily rising and outweighing resistance, other things being equal, then their effective reacting will wane inversely to the counteracting-index-weighted-by-an-exponent-greater-than-unity."

Just as expected by the generalized harmonic curve, the effective reacting (knowers) varied inversely with the intervening distance weighted by an exponent of nearly 2 (i.e., $L^x = L^{1.8}$).

K. *Negative Powers clan* ($\Delta = A^{-a}$) of reactants curves (Fig. 2)- observed order in divided diffusing.

The last four submodels can be portrayed as arrays of a matrix which shows action and reaction, telling and hearing, by fiat as man-made laws.

Key: Solid lines show the curve expected by the hypothesis, ${}_2A_h$; x's show observed data (means), ${}_2A_0$.

A = all-or-none item-actant (=1,0); ${}_1A$ = preactants (= tellings or tellers); ${}_2A$ = reactants (= hearings or hearers). Since preacts are steady, ${}_1A = T$ and $\Delta = A^{-a} \equiv T^{-a}$.

$\Sigma\Delta$ = an additive increment in reacts; t = number of unit periods = n = number of preactants (1 per period).

k = the "potency constant," a social force of 1 act per actor per period per period (from scratch).

r = a closeness of fit index, the intraclass correlation of hypothesized vs. observed increments of reaction.

Summary: (Figure 2): These four graphs visualize, in sets of people and periods the significant (5% level) and close ($r^2 > .9$) fits of these four reactants hypotheses to four sets of observed communicating of items. These four hypotheses predict reaction from given preactants under preconditions. They expect in general: "If one or all n preactants (i.e., tellings or tellers) are steadily followed by k equal reactants then the diffusing of that reaction is predictable by the corresponding reactants index, ${}_2A_h$, as hypothesized."

DATA* FOR FIGURE 2

Lineau Curve Data
(under 100% control)

Abscissa (tellings)	Frequencies of Hearings Expected ΣΔ	Observed ΣΔ
10	10	10
9	9	9
8	8	8
7	7	7
6	6	6
5	5	5
4	4	4
3	3	3
2	2	2
1	1	1

$r_{ic} = 1.00$

Logarithmic Curve Data

Abscissa (leaflet ratio)	Frequencies of Hearings Expected Δ	Observed Δ
1/4	25.2	25.2
1/2	34.0	37.4
1/1	42.9	30.1
2/1	51.7	44.1
4/1	60.6	63.4
8/1	69.4	71.8
16/1	78.3	82.4
32/1	87.1	87.9

$r_{ho} = .97 \; p(x^2) > .05$

Harmonic Curve Data

Abscissa (removed)	Frequencies of Hearings Expected ΣΔ	Observed ΣΔ
0	5.12	5.12
1	2.56	3.20
2	1.71	2.36
3	1.28	2.00
4	1.02	1.00
5	.85	1.00

$r_{ho} = .99 \; p(x^2) > .05$

Squared Harmonic Curve Data

Abscissa (distance)	Frequencies of Hearings Expected Δ	Observed Δ
1	61.9	61.9
2	17.8	14.2
3	8.6	9.5
4	5.1	4.8
5	3.4	4.8
6	2.5	2.4
7	1.9	2.4

$r_{ho} = .997 \; p(x^2) > .85$

*All data are from the "Revere Studies on Interaction" volume.

TABLE 2

The Negative Powers or
Hyperbolic Model for Four Reactant Curves - A "Fiat Case" - $[\Delta = A^{-a}]$
defining four further laws of communication

n = t → ↓	A time schedule of broadcasting with equal opportunity						Totals†
	1st wk.	2nd wk.	3rd wk.	4th wk.		tth wk.	
1st candidate	1 hour	1/2 hr.	1/3 hr.	1/4 hr.	---	1/t hr.	log t/1
2nd candidate		1/2 hr.	1/3 hr.	1/4 hr.	---	1/t hr.	log t/2
3rd candidate			1/3 hr.	1/4 hr.	---	1/t hr.	log t/3
4th candidate				1/4 hr.	---	1/t hr.	log t/4
---	---	---	---	---	---	---	---
nth candidate						1/t hr.	log t/t-1
Totals →	1 hour	1 hour	1 hour	1 hour		1 hour	t hours

†Euler's correction for discrete units is needed when t is small as here. Here:

1. the "constant submodel" predicts (bottom row) a *set* of TIME elements (1 hr./ wk.);

2. the "linear submodel" predicts (left column) a *sum* of steadily added ACTORS, e.g., candidates to date.

3. the "harmonic submodel" predicts (top row), as an *inverse product*, the ACTS per actor in minute units.

4. the "logarithmic submodel" predicts (top right cell) a *power* of the TRANSACTION cumulated for the first candidate;

5. the "squared harmonic submodel" predicts (diagonal cells), as a larger negative power, the $1/t^2$ hours of hearing the new teller relative to total teller hours to date (=t), i.e., $t/t^2 = 1/t$;

6. the "compounded log harmonic submodel" predicts (right column), as a positive and negative power, the total (t) hours to date of hearing each teller in turn (and also the total of weekly listening hours in the bottom row, as a check).*

[1] Note how these four negative powers clan of models are generated by building up the four sides or outer arrays of the matrix Table 2. They exemplify thus the four "semiocycles" or semiotic power levels which are operationally defined by our reiteration rule (Ref. 16) for basic formulating of all semiotic and scientific and social laws. They also progressively enlarge the transaction or process modeled by cumulatively compounding the basic dimensions of Time, Actors (=People here), and Acts.

The relations of these submodels to this hyperbolic model for message diffusing is thus seen from Table 2 to be that of an array or vector to a larger matrix. The relation can also be described as that of subsystems to a supersystem; that of internally structured factors to a still more complexly structured product; that of regular social subprocesses in a larger social process; or just parts within a whole moving "item structure."

III.

Formulas Forecasting Reactants, A^a

We submit that these models, sketched above, from Project Revere, may be ordered into a system or theory. We name this model or operationally defined theory "the reactants model" and shall state it algebraically by the dimensional formula [$\triangle = A^{\pm a}$]. This will have subsystems, or subprocesses in diffusing, such as the present submodels sketched above, according as the governing exponent, $a = \pm^{(0, 1, 2, 3, \ldots)}$.

A. *Four variables defined*

Let us start to derive these models with *a set of n subsets of N elements.* The reactants model uses just three subsets—called "basic dimensions" of behavioral sciences, namely, sets of: *acts, people,* and *times.* Their compounds in item-structures can be shown in algebraic theorems to order some probable diffusing acts of men in time as laws or constant "if—then" statements.

These subsets (of the universal set of all elements) may be acted on and combined in any of the ways[4] studied in the behavioral sciences or the semiotic sciences (logic, mathematics, language, communications, etc.). Our reactants model is a subsystem or submodel of our transact model, (Ref. 13) which is in turn a submodel of our panactants model. (Refs. 7, 10)

Since science has to do with predicting, we start by splitting the set of spans into earlier and later subsets. Taking these two subsets of times together with the set of acts gives the products

[4] Our reiteration rule orders *all* these acts on sets. (See Ref. 16).

(i.e., intersets) called "preacts" or "reacts." (See Fig. 3.) The product or joint occurrence of preacts and reacts we call the set of "*inter*acts." Their further products with the subset of "people" gives the (sub-sub) sets named "preactors," "reactors," "interactors." Their still further products with the subset of acts called "speech acts" (taken here as a basic term) gives our four chief communication variables as sets of "*tellings*" and "*hearings*" (or "*tellers*" and "*hearers*"). Finally the set of "either acts or actors" (i.e., their sum or union) is called the set of "actants.'

FIGURE 3
Production of the Reactants Models
As Sums and Products of Three Primitive Sets:
Acts of *People* at *Times*
$=A^{\circ}_{A}$ $=P^{\circ}$ $=T^{\circ}$

Times, T

Sums (unions) of 2 row cells ↓	EARLIER, ${}_1T$	LATER, ${}_2T$	Products (i.e., intersects) of the 2 row cell entries ↓
Acts, A_A (Speech acts) A_S ($=A^{\circ}S$)	Preacts ${}_1A_A$ (Tellings)	Reacts ${}_2A_A$ (Hearings)	interacts ${}_{12}A_A$ ("Tell-hears")
ACTORS, Ap ($=A^{\circ}P$) = Acts • People (Speech actors)	Preactors ${}_1A_P$ (Tellers)	Reactors ${}_2A_P$ (Hearers)	Interactors ${}_{12}A_P$ (Teller-Hearers)
Actants, A (Speech actants)	Preactants ${}_1A$ (Speech pre-actants)	Reactants ${}_2A$ (Speech re-actants)	Interactants ${}_{12}A$ (Speech interactants)

Terms in parentheses in the cells denote communicational acts defined as an algebraic "set-product," or behavioral joint occurrences, of the cell's set of actants *and* the set of speech acts.

The zero exponent denotes "a set of elements" of the sort named by the base letter.

B. *Eight hypotheses formalized*

Using the definitions above, the hypotheses coming forth as best proven from Project Revere will be formally restated below. Their phrasing is aimed to state the exact conditions (within sampling limits) under which each submodel can be observed, predicted, and applied in science.

A "communication version" of the eight reactants hypotheses follows:

1. The LINEAR hypothesis expects:
"If items are told one per period, and heard with like-chance, then a linear curve predicts that *collective diffusing.*"

2. The LOGARITHMIC hypothesis expects:
"If tellings shrink inversely with time and are cumulatively heard, with like-chance, then logarithmic curves predict *self-competitive diffusing.*"

3. The HARMONIC hypothesis expects:
"If rival tellers increase steadily, and are heard with like-chance, then a harmonic curve predicts this 'diluted' or *countered diffusing.*"

4. The SQUARED HARMONIC hypothesis expects:
"If tellers increase steadily, while hearings decrease steadily, then a squared harmonic curve may predict *doubly countered diffusing.*"

5. The NORMAL hypothesis expects:
"If any half of a set of people hears each item with like-chance, then a normal probability distribution predicts *chance-like diffusing.*"

6. The EXPONENTIAL hypothesis expects:
"If people hear one item repeated, with like-chance in each period, then a waning exponential growth curve of increments predicts *compounding diffusion.*"

7. The LOGISTIC hypothesis expects:
"If people communicate an item (1) steadily, (2) in pairs, (3) with like-chance, then a logistic growth curve predicts dyadic *cooperative diffusing.*"

8. The third and fourth moment submodels, though untested as yet, seem promising for modeling diffusion among believers vs. disbelievers, and among friends vs. foes.

The General Reactants Hypothesis expects, then:

> "If people tell item messages steadily with like-chance in specified structurings, then specified curves predict, within sampling limits, the resulting diffusion."

For comparison with the "communication version" above, a "process version" of the reactants hypotheses which may be more generally termed an "action," follows:

1. If to a steady process of one preact at a time, people react *proportionally,* then a LINEAR curve foretells their reacting.
2. If to a steady process of one preact at a time people react *inversely,* then a HARMONIC curve foretells their reacting.
3. If to a steady process of one preact at a time people react in *inverse* amount and *cumulatively,* then a LOGARITHMIC curve nearly[5] foretells their reacting.
4. If to a steady process of one preact at a time, people react in *inverse* amount and *increasingly* so, then a SQUARED HARMONIC curve foretells their relative reacting.
5. If to a steady process of one preact at a time, people react *jointly to any half,* then a NORMAL curve foretells their probable "multiplex" reacting.
6. If to a steady process of one preact at a time, people react *repeatedly,* then an EXPONENTIAL curve foretells the probable "mass" reacting.
7. If to a steady process of one preact at a time, people with equal opportunity react *partly paired off,* then a LOGISTIC curve foretells the probable "social" reacting.
8. If to a steady process of one preact at a time, people with equal opportunity react *fully paired off,* then a GOMPERTZ curve foretells the probable "social" reacting.
9. If people react according to a function of steady preacts (such as item tellings), that function foretells their reacting (item hearings) at, or up to, any time.

Note these models have one shared condition which is paraphrased above as "with like-chance" for all or "with equal op-

[5] Euler's correction for discrete class-intervals is needed for less than about ten periods.

portunity." Underlying these overlapping provisos of "equable" conditions is our larger semiotic theory of elemental causation: Every transaction includes its *context-in-time*.[6] The causes of mass diffusion are legion. If observable, causal variables are controlled, then left over causal elements follow the regularities of sets of elements. This plurality of causal items for an instance of diffusion can be looked at in three degrees of its closeness-to-farness in time as follows:

1. As the increments in hearing, one after the other, each of which may affect the next increment by chance and which when added up in the negative powers clan, or multiplied together in the positive powers clan, constitute the whole diffusion process; or

2. As the foregoing increments in telling, each of which alone comes before its effect (such as each word told and then heard) but all together are just about at the same time during the hour's broadcast. These increments in telling (the preacts) happen here in an observable ratio (k in the linear submodel, for example) to the increments in hearing; or

3. As the further back events or larger social causes for the choices of particular broadcasters and topics talked on and for the listeners' amount of listening, etc.

These more remote social causes, #3, are not dealt with by the reactants models which are stated in terms of the more immediate causal factors (1) and (2).

C. *Reactants submodels formulated*

1. *Defining the sets of items.* We start developing the equations which specify the whole reactants model in the exact language of algebra by taking as given: *a set of n subjects of N elements.* The three dimensional subsets studied here may be expressed, with zero exponents denoting "a set of—," as:

A set of acts, A° (any events observed as all-or-none).
A set of people, P° (any human doers of the acts)
A set of unit-times, T° (each of any specified, but equal, length of

[6] We define a "transaction" as *a recorded human action-in-full-context* full enough to predict its recurrence under recurring conditions.

time from 0 to infinity) with two subsets of: "earlier times," ${}_1T°$, or "later times," ${}_2T°$; and using these pre-subscripts as adjectives we write "${}_1A$" for "earlier acts" or "preacts" and "${}_2A$" for "reacts," etc.

Then the products and sums of sets define the set of compounded elements as detailed above.

2. *The negative powers clan of submodels.* The equations below (Table 3) specify the transactions or behavior-in-situations where the amount of reaction is equal to the number of preactants when operated on (i.e., "structured") as given below for each submodel. The last column of Table 3 shows the finite differences from time to time which add up to yield the growth curve of diffusion. These are the dimensional formulas which define and systematize the "negative-power submodels," of the reactants model.

Note how the purpose of this paper—to order our data by means of a family of well-known curves—is partly fulfilled in the four deltas or growth increments. These four rates of diffusing an item

TABLE 3

The Negative Powers or Hyperbolic Clan of Reactants Submodels

Hyp.	Name of curve	Cumulated Equation	Operations in deriving	Definitive dimensional "difference equation"
1	Linear	${}_2A^1 = k\ {}_1A^1$	reaction equals constant preactions	$[\Delta = A^{-0}]$
2	Logarithmic	${}_2A^1 = k \sum_1^p A^{-1}$ $\doteq k \log {}_1A$	reaction equals summed inverse preactions	$[\Delta = A^{-1}]$
3	Harmonic	${}_2A^{\mathring{1}} = k\ {}_1A_P^{-1}$	reaction equals inverse preactors	$[\Delta = A^{-2}]$
4	Squared harmonic	${}_2A^1 = k\ {}_1A_P^{-2}$	reaction equals squared inverse preactors	$[\Delta = A^{-3}]$

or unit-act of men in time, form a regular series of increasingly negative exponents: $\triangle = A^{-(0,\,1,\,2,\,3,)}$.

3. *The positive powers, or moments, clan of submodels.* The equations below in Table 4 give the transactions in which the

TABLE 4

The Positive Powers or Momental Clan of Reactants Submodels

Hyp.	Name of curve	Power form of equation	Probability form	Operations in deriving	Definitive "basal factor," $\triangle_{lg}$, equation
5	Normal	$_2Ap = {_1}\overline{A^0}^t$	$= (p_0 + q_0)^t$	reactors equal a power of the zeroth central moment of the n preacts	$[\triangle_{lg} = A^{+0}]$
6	Exponential	$_2Ap = {_1}\overline{A^1}^t$	$= (1 - p_0)^t$ $= q^t$	reactors equal a power of the first raw moment of 1 preact	$[\triangle_{lg} = A^{+1}]$
7	Logistic	$_2Ap = {_1}\overline{A^2}^{(t)}$	$= (1 - p_0^2)^t$ $= (p_t q_t)^{(t)}$	reactors equal the chain product or storchastic power of the second central moment from 1 preactor	$[\triangle_{lg} = A^{+2}]$
8	Double binomial	$_2Ap = {_1}A\overline{p^3}^t$	$= (q - p)_t^t$ $= (1\text{-}2p)$	reactors equal a power of the third central moment of n preactors	$[\triangle_{lg} = A^{+3}]$

Some compounded submodels studied in Project Revere are:

Hyp.	Name of curve	Power form of equation	Probability form	Operations in deriving	Definitive "basal factor," $\triangle_{lg}$, equation
9	Gompertz	$_2Ap = {_1}A\overline{p}^{-2^t}$	$= q_0^{2^t}$	reactors equal a bits power, 2^t, of a first raw moment of n preactors	$[\triangle_{lg} = A^{+1} \cdot A^{-1}]$
10	Harmonic logistic	$_2Ap = {_1}Ap$	$= \dfrac{(p_t q_t)^{(t)}}{t}$	reactors equal the product of the logistic and the harmonic submodels	$[\triangle_{lg} = A^{+2} \cdot A^{-1}]$

number of reactors is equal to the number of preactants when operated on or structured in the six ways shown. The last column exhibits the factors (or logarithmic differences, ∇_{lg}) which *multiply together* to produce the growth curve of diffusion. Again note that this family of diffusion curves is ordered by their regularly increasing exponents or statistical moments, $\triangle_{lg} = A^{+(0, 1, 2, 3,)}$.

Certain symmetries in the moments clan should be noted.

a. The zeroth moment predicts for *persons.*
b. The first moment predicts for *plurels.*
c. The second moment predicts for dyadic *groups.*
d. The third moment is not studied, but seems to predict for opposed plurels.
e. The fourth moment is not studied, but seems to predict for opposed dyads.
f. The first three moments predict "pro-acting" and the last two moments predict "contra-acting."
g. The odd moments predict "mechanical" spread in plurels; the even moments predict "social" diffusion in groups.
h. Linear and normal curves are more important than harmonic and logistic curves. I.e., the lower moments seem more prevalent than the higher moments.

Some applications of these formulas or examples of these processes are:

a. The zeroth moment may predict the normal probability of each child in a school class learning n new facts $(p+q)^t$;
b. The first moment may predict how a radio audience learns a new repeated fact with exponentially waning probability, (q^t);
c. The second moment may predict how a set of dance partners or telephone communicators learn a new fact with logistic probability $(pq)^{(t)}$;
d. The third moment may predict how believers and disbelievers learn a news item with "binomial difference" probability $(q\text{-}p)^t$;
e. The fourth moment may predict how two hostile factions, if meet-

TABLE 5

Development of the Moments and Basic Operations

Central moments ↓	Semiotic Cycle 0 of sets = $[A^{\overline{0}}]$ called "kinds of action"	Semiotic Cycle I, II of Sums and Ratios = $[A^{1,2}]$ called "probabilities of action"	Semiotic Cycle III of Powers $[A^{at}]$ called "growth of action"
$\overline{A^{+0}} = \sum^{P} A^0/P$	$p^0 \cup q^0$ set p or set q	p^1+q^1, alternative probability	$(p+q)^t$ binomial and normal submodel
$A^{+T} = \sum^{P} A^1/P$	$\sim p \cup \sim q$ neither set p nor set q	0, null probability	0^t constancy submodel
$\overline{A^{+2}} = \sum^{P} A^2/P$	$p^0 \cap q^0$ both set p and set q	$p^1 \times q^1$ joint probability	$(pq)^{(t)}$ logistic submodel
$\overline{A^{+3}} = \sum^{P} A^3/po^2$	$p^0 \subset q^0$ set p implies set q	$q^1 - p^1$ difference probability	$(q-p)^t$ difference binomial submodel
$\overline{A^{+4}} = \sum^{P} A^3/Po^4$	$p^0 = q^0$ i.e., set p equals set q	$1/p^1q^1$ = an inverse of a joint probability (in variance units)	$(1/pq-3)^t$ an inverse logistic function

† These "semiotic cycles" of sets, sums, products, and powers are defined by the Reiteration Rule (Ref. 16).

in pairs, may learn a partisan item with "logistic difference" probabilities $(1\text{-}3pq)^{t}$.[7]

Development of the first raw moment $\overline{^{0,}A^1}$ involves: in Cycle $\overline{O}$ asserting a set, also its complement; in Cycle I, a probability, also its complement; and in Cycle III, a growth curve building up

[7] Of the many other symmetries emerging from the momental clan of submodels, a fundamental syntactic one should be noted since it generates the momental submodels. The first five statistical moments, $A^{\overline{0,1,2,3,4}}$, when observed at the qualitative level of sets (see Refs. 16 and 25), involve respectively the five logical constants ($\cup \sim \cap \subset =$); and when observed at the quantitative level of numbers, involve the equivalent mathematical operators ($+ \; 0 \; \times \; - \; =$ etc.) and also define the five elementary forms of probability; and at their power levels become the five momental submodels for diffusion, as spelled out in Table 5.

as a power of the number, t, of time periods of intra-action.

4. *Comparison of the two clans of submodels.* Further features which systematize the two clans in symmetrical contrasts are:

The negative powers clan:	The positive powers clan:
1a. had additive increments, i.e., △ is an addend;	1b. has multiplicative increments, i.e., △ is a factor, or log addend;
2a. predicts the variable *number* of subsets of *hearings,* each subset being of size k;	2b. predicts the variable proportion, p, in just 1 subset (and its complement) of *hearers;*
3a. is computed as a *negative power of a sum* of n subsets, each with 1 element;	3b. is computed as an *averaged positive power* of the elements in 1 subset;
4a. has 1 in every cell of its matrix;	4b. has 1 or 0 in every cell of its matrix;
5a. deals with moments *between subsets;*	5b. deals with moments *within* one subset;
6a. deals, in short, with *many subsets* with *one* interactant *element* in each;	6b. deals, in short, with *one subset* with *many* interactant elements.

D. *Reactants model in seven algebraic forms*

Let us now bring the foregoing hypotheses and their equations together in a prose paragraph and a simple algebraic formula, [$\triangle = A^a$], for the whole reactants model which will be restated in each of seven alternative forms below. This is our systemed answer from Project Revere to the Air Force's question: How fast will an item message diffuse through a set of people under specified preconditions? These conditions should be highly general (and so apply to any message, population, situation, or culture), highly prevalent (and so predictable within probability limits), and highly operational (and so controllable by leaflet operators).

Form 1. The "item-structured" formula—states the local averaged rate, k, and general form, A^a, of the diffusing or spreading of an item message.

$$\triangle \text{ (Delta)} = k\ A^{\overline{+a}} \quad (A = 1, 0); a = +(0, 1, 2, 3)$$

This is an algebraic product representing a behavioral joint occurrence of two factors, k and A, as follows:

$\triangle$ represents a net increment in the hearers in a time unit, i.e., the number of new hearers per teller and unit-period.

k is the "potency" parameter, observed as the average number of new hearers per teller in a period. It summarizes the "potency" or interest of the particular population for the particular message in the particular situation.

$A^{\pm a}$ is the "structuring" or "shape of curve."

This factor transcends the given message, people, and culture and is produced solely by universal and basic givens of the number and combination of ACTANTS ACTING WITH LIKE-CHANCE. For this reason, we see the formula, $\triangle = kA^{\overline{\pm a}}$, as stating a basic group of "laws of reactants" in behavioral science, and, analogously, in all other sciences. This reactants formula summarizes all the submodels or curves described in this paper on the reactants models. The A^a represents the invariant factor (i.e., shape of curve or law) in the diffusing situation, while k represents the highly variant potency factor (i.e., slope, or time rate, or local influences).

Form 2. The *"dimensional" formula—concerning the categories which are basic to behavioral science.* The simplest summary (with neglect of detail) for the multi-form reactants model is its dimensional formula (Refs. 2, 3, 7, 10), namely:

$$[\triangle = A^a]$$

This formula says in prose that a unit increase of diffusing or spreading is given by a unit all-or-none actant when "structured" by raising it to the ath power (and neglecting further operations of averaging etc.).

This dimensional formula orders the eight regular forms for acts of actors when diffusing over time as a growth (or along any other dimension of the transaction). It implies a compound unit *transact* as it is a recorded core act in the context of its actors and successive periods under equable and other specified structuring conditions.

Form 3. The "integrated" or "exponent formulas"—concerning consequences of diffusion.

In the negative powers clan, $\triangle = A^{-a}$, one may see:

"a *collective process,*" in the linear curve, A^{-0}
"a *competitive process,*" in the log curve, A^{-1}
"a *countered process,*" in the harmonic curve, A^{-2}
"a *doubly countered process,*" in the squared harmonic curve, A^{-3}

In the positive powers clan, $\triangle = A^{+a}$, one has:

"a *chance process,*" in the normal curve, $A^{\overline{+0}}$
"a *compounding process,*" in the exponential curve, $A^{\overline{+1}}$
"a *cooperative process,*" in the logistic curve, $A^{\overline{+2}}$
"a *counter-vailing process,*" in the difference binominal curve, $A^{\overline{+3}}$
"a *conflictive process,*" in the negative logistic curve, $A^{\overline{+4}}$
"a *cybernetic process,*" in the Gompertz curve, $\overline{A^{1}}^{+2}$

Another use of reactants models in ogive form is as a baseline for group ongoings from which to measure deviant cases due to the many "masking" or "nonchance, orderly variables" in which sociologists studying group behavior are usually most interested.

Form 4. The rectified formulas—concerning contents of diffusion.

Suppose one has observed the percentages of a population diffused up to successive time points, t. What submodel fits or describes these data best? A rectified equation or graph provides a rough but easily seen answer.

A rectified equation is one that re-expresses the integral equation as a straight line, plotting cumulated diffusion up to date against that date. To test quickly how well a specific submodel here fits given diffusion data, plot those data *in log units* against time on an arithmetic scale. The slope of this plotted straight line gives the mean speed of diffusion as:

$$p' / t = k_s.$$

Form 5. The regression formula—concerning closeness of fit. If a more exact test of the closeness of fit of a hypothesized submodel to the observed diffusion increments of knowers is wanted, the correlation between model and data, theory and fact, may be computed. As a working standard of acceptable descriptive fits, we required the intraclass of increments correlation of hypothesis with observation to be over .9, and also to be significantly different from 0 at the 5 percent level, throughout Project Revere. Thus, as Fig. 1 shows ,the eight reactants submodels each correlated well above $r=.9$, and even above $r=.99+$ in the controlled experiments.[8] This means in terms of the regression equation that at least 81 percent and up to 99 percent of the observed variance of the spread was explained by the model. The regression equation reads;

$$\Delta_o = r_{\Delta h \Delta o} \, {}^{o}\Delta_h \; (\pm\sigma_h \sqrt{1-r^2})$$

where h denoted hypothesized, and o denotes observed, increments.

Form 6. The ratio formula—concerning causes of diffusing. The diffusion transaction when completed means that a population has been changed in an overall period from nonknowers to knowers in respect to an item of knowledge. The immediate cause of this net result can be looked at as the many acts of telling and hearing. The ratio formula reads:

$$\Sigma\Delta = T^{-a} \; (=n^{-a}) \quad \text{and} \quad {}_2A = \Sigma\overset{T}{\Delta} = \Sigma T^{T-a}$$

This formula cleanly separates the two clans of submodels thus: The negative powers clan deal with the number, n, of sets, so the numerator is unity, $p_a=1$. The positive powers clan deal with the proportion, p, of elements (of one set), so the denominator

[8] The correlation of increments between classes, ${}^{r}\Delta\,\Delta$, in time was used as the index of fit for three reasons. It is more exacting, versatile, and causal than the Pearsonian r. We defined causation operationally as: "A is a cause of B to the extent that changes in A are correlated with later changes in B in the absence of any correlated changes in the context, C, so that: Correlation as a percentage index of causation: $100r^2 \; \Delta_A\Delta \cdot {}_B\Delta_C \rightarrow 100\%$.

is unity, $n^a = 1$. In the composite models such as the harmonic and Gompertz neither n nor p are unity.

Form 7. The "temporal" formulas—about the pure process of diffusing. A seventh transformation or variant algebraic version of the reactants model states it most usefully as a pure process or steady on-going in time.

In terms of the time elapsed, T, the negative powers clan can then be most simply expressed as:

$$\overset{t}{\Sigma}\lg(\Delta_{lg}) = \sum_{1}^{t} \lg({}_{2}A^{\overline{+a}}), \text{ or } p_t = ({}_{2}A^{\bar{a}})^{(t)}$$

The positive powers clan can likewise be expressed in its "cumulated temporal form" as the proportion diffused p_t, up to the tth unit time period as:

$$\Delta = p_a/n^a$$

This states the reactants model as a steady stochastic development (denoted by the exponent in parenthesis) where each successive change in unit time governs the next change in unit time.

E. *Item-structured super-models a-forming*

To understand this reactants model fully, one needs a statement of its background. Our contribution (which we call "item structuring") is a semiotic model which produced this reactants system with its eight subsystems. Since a full statement of it cannot be made in one article (see Refs. 1-29), only a glimpse is possible here, stating how the reactants system is one item of fruitage from our dimensional analysis (Refs. 2, 3) in its 1960 form of item-structuring models.

Our semiotic modeling is meant to help build a system of rules useful in making highly changeless, or even constant item structures. It is aimed to further the making or manufacturing of models with ever-higher generality, prevalence, and operationality in behavioral science. Every item structure here is a fully specified and duplicatable compounding of both syntactic and matching behavioral operations. The syntactic operations on symbols are such as adding, multiplying, etc., all of which seem to us can be made and ordered entirely by the reiteration rule (Ref. 16). Each syntactic, or largely methodological, operation is to be matched, 1-to-1, by a corresponding behavioral, or largely substantive, operation.

The syntactic-behavioral operations of modeling build up from elements reiterated into sets. Syntactically viewed, these sets of elements are elemental speech acts called "namings" (as in every word) which combine into sentences, formulas, and all speech. Behaviorally viewed, these words in a model are to be closely matched by the things-named as observable items of action-in-context and as compounded structures of items called "models." An example of such an item-structure is "propaganda" when thought of extensionally and seen quantitatively as "item-messages-told-and-heard" and structured in the reactants model for "spreading item messages among people in time" as stated in detail by the formulas, tables, and prose paragraphs of this paper and summarized by:

$$A^a.$$

These item structures, or behavioral models specified in algebraic formulas, are expected—as our "semiotic hypothesis of item structuring"—to help social scientists more and more to order their scientific methodology by rules for thinking more extensionally, quantitatively, correlationally, systematizingly and so, more testably (Refs. 8,9,12,14,15,18,19,20,22-29). The output of such thinking is here foretold to be an augmenting system of more and more useful, proven, and highly constant "if-then" statements, some of which will ripen into sociological laws.

This semiotic hypothesis of item structuring will be proven in the long run insofar as it increasingly yields a more *exact and predictive science of behavior.*

IV.

Evaluation by Three Criteria

Let us turn from statement of the reactants models to judging them by the three criteria that were set as objectives at the start of Project Revere.[9]

A. *How general are the reactants models?*

1. The models' substantive behavior of observees is spreading messages—telling anything whatever—communicative behavior. In form, the units of diffusing were made to be highly general by neglecting the meanings in the item messages and by observing them only as all-or-none acts, the electronic computer's binary variable, or the layman's present-or-absent item—which we call an "It" for "item." In content, let a unit-transact be standardized for greatest generality as "1 recorded Act of 1 person in 1 Time period" under unit-indices of context ($=C^o=1$).

2. The methodological behavior of observers in the reactants models consists of highly general *"item structuring"* or modeling from sets of elements. This means building (a) the formula, (b) the referent behavior, through these stages:

(O) Listing all elements into
(I) Adding these SETS into
(II) Multiplying these SUMS into
(III) Self-multiplying these PRODUCTS into POWERS

Compounding these syntactic operations and their inverses in specified ways yields any formula that can be expressed in logic or mathematics. Then we aim to make any model in behavioral science (Refs. 2, 3, 16) expressible as the behaviors named by the symbols for variables and their combinative operations in the formulas.

3. The complementary behavior of all other than the diffused observees and the research observers in the reactants model consists of any changes or varyings in the context of the core act of diffusing which are correlated to that act. Such contextual change subdivide into the larger vs. smaller, the observed vs. unobserved, the orderly vs. chance variables, the "masking factors" vs. the

[9] It should also be noted that the models satisfy well the three methodological criteria of reliability, validity and predictivity.

"multiplex elements," etc. These reactants models order multiplexes of elements, i.e., compounds of sets of n subsets of N elements.

B. *How prevalent are the reactants models?*

In judging these reactants models what should be noted about how often they occur in human affairs? What may be the actual vs. the potential frequency of occurrence of the models and of the behaviors they model?

1a. *Actual use of reactants formulas* now seems to us rare, partial, or mostly implicit or even unconscious. Thus the normal probability formula is dealt with whenever the examination scores of a large school class are expected to be normally distributed. Of course, all the eight reactant submodels are familiar formulas that are long since in limited or partial use in special fields.

1b. *Potential use of reactants formulas* offer the richest results in predicting behavior, we believe, if applied to mass behaviors such as in mass communications. Here we suggest trial in situations which *a priori* seem to involve structuring ratios that are either (1) one to one, or (2) one to many, or (3) many to many, among appropriate sets of acts and reacts, actors and reactors. These three structuring ratios yield respectively (1) the normal probability model as in school classes, (2) the waning exponential growth model as in broadcasting, and (3) the logistic interaction model as in conversational pairs.

All this means to us that laws of human mass behavior are likely to be found by reobserving what people say and do in extensional and dynamic terms of combinations and ratios among sets of interactant elements.

2a. *Actual occurrence of the behaviors* ordered here is too vast a field for brief review. (Refs. 1-29 treat it more fully.)

2b. *The potential prevalence of behaviors* fitting reactants models depends mostly on the researchers' behaviors in thinking extensionally instead of intensionally; i.e., in terms of sets of listed elements instead of class-properties. When the intensional adjective "chance" was replaced by the extensional adjective "multiplex" (meaning "a countable set of many, small, uncorrelated elements") a word often hiding our ignorance was made into a name for a law-abiding mechanism. The same hold for using the extensional word "polled" opinion in place of the intensional word "public" opinion.

C. *How operational are the reactants models?*

In judging these reactants models what can be said about their three subsets of semiotic operations, namely:

(a) syntactic operations relating symbols to symbols?
(b) semantic operations relating symbols to their symboled referents?
(c) pragmatic operations relating symbols, the symboled, and the symbolizers?

Syntactically, one can deduce all the reactants formulas (and many more formulas as needed) from the assumed SET OF n SUBSETS OF N ELEMENTS by the syntactic acts of logic and mathematics (Refs. 20,22,24,25)

Semantically, one can induce all the reactants models using only operational definitions as shown above in IIIA. The five basic words—"acts" of "actors" at "earlier" or "later" "times"—have one-to-one correspondence between their standard referents and new applications of the words by most users in particular situations. In short, these words can be shown to be highly reliable by controlled experiments such as were reported in our *Dimensions of Society* for the whole system of sociological concepts.

Pragmatically, the leaflet operator can get messages spread to the extent that he can control its conditions. He can reckon on, and increasingly manipulate:

1. normal distribution,
2. exponential growth,
3. logistic growth,

4. third moment and fourth moment modifiers,
5. linear growth,
6. harmonic counteracting,
7. logarithmic diminishing returns,
8. Gompertz feedback.

D. *Conclusions on reactants modeling*

The reactants models given above are Project Revere's answer to one of the Air Force's first questions: How fast will a leaflet message spread under given conditions? The answer from this research is: The speed of diffusion is predictable by the *reactants formula* for successive increments in the percent of the people hearing the message in a unit of time. This reactants formula is a compact algebraic statement of the highly catholic "reactants model" which is part of our operationally defined theory of stochastic or "multiplex" or probabilistic causation. The reactants model is, in turn, a special case of our highly general "transactants model" (Ref. 13). The reactants formula is aimed to help describe and explain, to predict and govern, given structures of the *probable acts and wants of men* in time and space under circumstances having nearly equal opportunity. (Ref. 25)

These eight reactants models seem to us likely to become well tested and eventually known as scientific laws with the following features:

1. High invariance—the consequent growth curve will *always* be observed *insofar as* the "if" conditions ("free and steady" acting) are fully and solely there, without masking.
2. High precision—within sampling limits, the growth curves should predict the course of the social process at hand to many decimal places.
3. High generality—The interactants may be any large sets of active elements in any field of deductive, empirical, or applied science. Hence the reactants models offer laws for social mechanics whenever the actors and acts are people communicating freely or otherwise interacting as given by $\triangle = \overline{A^a}$.

AUTHOR'S REFERENCES

1. Dodd, Stuart C. "A Theory for the Measurement of Some Social Forces," *The Scientific Monthly,* vol. XLIII, no. 1, no. 250, July, 1936.

2. ——. *Dimensions of Society.* Macmillan, 1942, 944 pp.

3. ——. *Systematic Social Science.* American University of Beirut, Social Science Series, no. 16, University of Washington Bookstore, Seattle, 1947, 788 pp.

4. ——. "The Interactance Hypothesis: A Gravity Model Fitting Physical Masses and Human Groups," *American Sociological Review,* vol. XV, no. 2, April, 1950.

5. ——. "Sociomatrices and Levels of Interaction—for dealing with plurels, groups, and organizations," *Sociometry,* vol. XIV, nos. 2, 3, May-August, 1951.

6. ——. "On All-or-None Elements and Mathematical Models for Sociologist," *American Sociological Review,* vol. XVII, no. 2, April, 1952.

7. ——. "Human Dimensions—A Re-search for Concepts to Integrate Thinking," *Main Currents in Modern Thought,* vol. IX, no. 4, August, 1953.

8. ——.Testing Message Diffusion in Controlled Experiments, Charting the Distance and Time Factors in the Interactance Hypothesis," American Socio-*logical Review,* vol. XVIII, no. 4, August, 1953.

9. ——. "Can the Social Scientist Serve Two Masters—an answer through experimental sociology," Proceedings of the Pacific Sociological Society, *Research Studies of the State College of Washington,* vol. XXI, no. 3, September, 1953.

10. ——. "A Dimensional System of Human Values," with Chahin Turabian, *Transactions Second World Congress of Sociology,* International Sociology Association, 1954, pp. 100-105.

11. ——. "Seven-Year Report, 1947-54," *Washington Public Opinion Laboratory,* University of Washington, Seattle, 1955, 31 pp.

12. ——. "Diffusion is Predictable: Testing probability models for laws of interaction," *American Sociological Review,* vol. XX, no. 4, August, 1955.

13. ——. "The Transact Model—a predictive and testable theory of social action, interaction and role-action," *Sociometry,* vol. XVIII, no. 4, December, 1955.

14. ——. "A Test of Message Diffusion by Chain Tags," *American Journal of Sociology,* vol. LXI, no. 5, March, 1956.

15. "Testing Message Diffusion in Harmonic Logistic Curves," *Psychometrika,* Vol. XXI, no. 2, June, 1956.

16. ——. "The Reiteration Rule—a cyclic system for syntax, neurograms, and all laws," AAAS, Society for General Systems Research Conference, December, 1956, and *Synthese,* March, 1959.

17. ——. "Conditions for Motivating Men—the valuance theory for motivating behaviors in any culture," *Journal of Personality,* vol. XXV, no. 4, June, 1957.

* Since the bibliography on these familiar submodels individually runs to hundreds of titles, only the author's contributions, cited in this paper, are listed here.

18. ——. "The Counteractance Model—for a resistive part of a whole interaction," *American Journal of Sociology,* vol. LXIII, no. 3, November, 1957.

19. ——. "A Power of Town Size Predicts its Internal Interacting—a controlled experiment relating the amount of an interaction to the number of potential interactors," *Social Forces,* vol. XXXVI, no. 2, December, 1957.

20. ——. "Formulas for Spreading Opinions—a report of controlled experiments on leaflet messages in Project Revere," *Public Opinion Quarterly,* Winter, 1958-59.

21. ——. "An Alphabet of Meanings—for the oncoming revolution in man's thinking," *Educational Theory,* vol. IX, no. 3, July, 1959.

22. ——. "How Random Interacting Organizes a Population—exploring a simple chance model to relate diffusion theory to information theory," *Synthese,* vol. XII, no. 1, March, 1960.

23. ——. With M. McCurtain. "The Logistic Law in Communication—Symposia Series no. 8, Nat'l. Inst. of Soc. & Beh. Sci., Washington, D.C., September, 1961.

24. ——. "The Momental Models for Diffusing Attributes," *Darshana,* Mora dabad, India, vol. II, no. 4, October, 1962.

25. ——. "How Momental Laws of Behavior Can Be Developed in Sociology—by deducing testable and predictive 'actance' models from transacts," *Synthese,* vol. XIV, no. 4, December, 1962.

26. ——. With M. McCurtain, "The Logistic Diffusion of Information Through Randomly Overlapped Cliques," *Operational Research Quarterly,* vol. 16, March 1965, pp. 51-63.

27. ——. Rejoinder to Nicosia re #26, October, 1965.

28. ——. With Wm. Pierce, "Three Momental Models for Predicting Message Diffusion," *Journal of Broadcasting.*

28. ——. With E. D. Rainboth and J. Nehnevajsa, "Revere Studies on Interaction," unpublished typescript, 1,000 pp., 1956 (deposited in the University of Washington Library).